EDITORIAL

If Calvinists believed in a multiplicity of transce_ responsible for the arts, we might expect him (or her) Predicament of the Scottish Writer', an evening or_ quantity of wine consumed that night, poured in a diffe_ a new volume of poetry. As the evening drew to a close, I felt it had been a blunder of the order of the Tate's famous display of bricks, not for being controversial or daring, but as someone declaimed, as the Cultural Non Event of the Year.

But let us not ask the Muse that such occasions be forever disallowed; nor reject it as an expensive publicity stunt. Let us not forget that wine is sacred to the Muse and that something can come both from nothing and from drinking too much.

Something did come out of that evening — a burning frustration that questions vital to Scottish culture were being trivialised, for, although such questions formed the backbone of the affair, the format was such that no serious discussion could emerge. In more bitter moments, I reflected that the predicament of Scottish writing was the complacent stupor into which those involved had sunk. Now we could congratulate ourselves smugly about sharing the predicament of being Scottish and entertaining certain 'Scottish' neuroses which made us somehow special. What angered me most was the lack of desire to get to the heart of the matter — not that we must always be serious about 'being Scottish', — all true humour and satire is based on serious observation.

My intention here is to provide a platform for serious discussion about the Predicament of Scotland, which is that of its writers also. I have asked writers to reflect quite uninhibitedly on the State of Scotland in their own fields — poetry, prose, journalism, criticism, folklore studies, theatre, philosophy, politics, education and publishing. What emerges is a wide range of opinion; there are some very moving statements, some very forceful, some overtly, some implicitly political, and covering a broad spectrum of politics.

There are two principal 'traps' into which Scottish culture, stemming from a small nation, can fall, and we manage to fall into both simultaneously. It can divide up into mutually antagonistic cliques who become so concerned to contradict and expose the other that objectivity is lost; or it can become too cosy, with no-one wanting to say anything which might offend. Both situations lead to the death of criticism, and to artistic sterility. I have tried to avoid both traps.

Many things emerge, particularly the urgency of the language problem for Scots and Gaelic, which need political action to ensure their survival. People must realise that the decision to use and preserve a language is political and cultural. Each contribution here confirms that politics and culture are inseparable. That this issue should appear at a time when a party opposed to Scottish autonomy, and to the ideology of most people in Scotland, is returned to power, is crushingly ironic.

The fate of Donald Stewart's bill to establish a geographical Gaidhealtachd is symbolic of the fate of Scottish culture under the present political structure. It is typical of the treatment of all matters of Scottish concern. This could have been the first step towards reversing the decline in all aspects of the Gaelic tradition. No such steps will be taken until a Scottish administration is established. Until then we must sit back powerlessly and watch the progressive dilution and disintegration of our culture, and most psychologically damaging of all is that sense of powerlessness, which breeds nothing but apathy.

The Predicament of Scotland, the State of Scotland, is a pre-occupation which is admittedly inward and introverted; some may say that it is no healthy preoccupation. But until there is a State of Scotland, we have no choice but be so obsessed. Would it were not so. But we can stop *talking* about the State of Scotland only when we are in a position to *do* something about it.

Joy Hendry

ALAN BOLD

AN OPEN LETTER ON THE CLOSED MIND

26th April, 1983

Dear Joy,

You ask me about the predicament of the Scottish writer. It's an interesting question and I suppose I must concede that the Scottish writer *is* in a predicament since the literary evidence of disarray is all around us. The predicament, of course, stems from the political situation: an English writer takes his (or her) national identity for granted, a Scottish writer has to assert it. This is what gives Scottish writing its argumentative quality, its belligerent mood, its assertive tone. Once Scotland had surrendered its independence the cultural implications were evident to the writers. Burns's words on the subject are well known to readers of *Chapman*, Scott's perhaps less so. That grand old Tory was considering the impact of his *Malachi Malagrowther* when he wrote in his Journal (of 14 March 1826) 'They are gradually destroying what remains of nationality, and making the country *tabula rasa* for doctrines of bold innovation. Their loosening and grinding down all those peculiarities which distinguished us as Scotsmen will throw the country into a state in which it will be universally turned to democracy, and instead of canny Saunders, they will have a very dangerous North British neighbourhood.' Burns and Scott, the literary Left and Right, unite in deploring the notion of North Britain. So it has been ever since and the spectacle of Scottish writing since 1707 has been a catalogue of complaint. Like it or not, and I often like it, Scottish literature has evolved into angry animal whose children — the Scottish writers — spend much of their time in vituperation.

All of this anger consumes an enormous amount of energy that perhaps might be used to better purpose. I say *perhaps* with good reason for some Scottish writers have made an immortal art of their anger. MacDiarmid most obviously. The sustained fury of *A Drunk Man Looks at the Thistle* (which leads at the end of the poem to an ineffable lyricism) — or the *Hymns to Lenin* for that matter — is a wonderful thing to behold. However MacDiarmid stressed the ideal of individuality, in all his work, and it must be recognised that he is unique. His anger is large, wholesome, healing. It has a purpose to it. George Douglas Brown is another Scottish writer who was consumed by hatred for an enemy when he wrote his masterpiece. Still, most Scottish writers have more in common with the Bodies that Brown created in *The House with the Green Shutters* than with the man who created them.

Remember the Bodies as they first appear, in the fifth chapter of Brown's sublime work? They are the most malicious gossips in literature, a swelling chorus seething with selfrighteous indignation. As Brown says, 'The genus 'bodie' is divided into two species: the 'harmless bodies' and the 'nesty bodies'. The bodies of Barbie mostly belonged to the second variety.' The same goes for literary Scotland. There is a love of intrigue, of congregating in gangs to do down other gangs. I have often observed the similarity between the territorial gangs who lurk in the antisocial architecture of cities and the little cliques of literature. The gang mentality is fundamentally fascist; it assumes (desperately in view of the conspicuous absence of actual achievement) that group-members are superior to those deemed to be outside the group. Therefore when kicking the head of someone not belonging to the group there is (so the gang mentality insists) morality in action. Similarly, literary cliques gather together to put the metaphorical boot into the head of someone they regard as a trespasser or an offensive outsider. The energy they expend in so doing so is entirely wasteful and it is rather nauseating to see the literary Bodies gathered together in territorial pubs where they form a chorus of malicious gossip.

When I lived in Edinburgh I was agonisingly aware of the predicament of being a Scottish writer because there was no way of escaping from it. Every coming together of the literary folk led to intrigue and argumentation. X would tell you that Y was up to no good because Z had said so: instead of discussing writing the conversation always dissected writers. This widespread literary vivisection was, and is, appallingly wasteful in terms of talent. I know because I certainly suffered from it as both participant and recipient. Reluctantly I found myself being drawn into purely personal assessments of other Scottish writers, and regularly I heard reports of what other Scottish writers had said about myself. The way this network of gossip works is by always assuming (1) that success is proof of evil intent, (2) that literary friendships are motivated by career contacts, (3) that Scots are not, in principle, to be trusted. All of this indicates that Scotland is still suffering from a monumental feeling of inferiority. As I see it the real predicament of being a Scottish writer is being surrounded by colleagues who have not understood that the artist's first responsibility is to himself. Unless he changes others he cannot change and the average Scottish writer is, catastrophically, a typical Scot.

The typical Scot, so far as such a creature is recognisable, is still recalling battles that were lost. The crucial moments of Scottish history are impressed on the national consciousness like dates cut deeply into tombstones. In 1513 the flowers of the forest were cut down at Flodden and Scots still lament the loss. In 1603 the Scottish crown was carried to England by James VI and the court played follow my leader. In 1699 an attempt to establish a Colony of Caledonia on Darien ended in disaster since the Scots only exported their insecurity. In 1707 the Scottish parliment committed legislative suicide and softened up Scotland, converted the country to defeatism. In 1746 the defeat of the clans at Culloden represented a cultural catastrophe and some say that Scotland lost its soul in the vicious acts of humiliation that followed. The Scot has been conditioned to regard himself as a loser and generally contrives to act like one. He is horribly unsure of himself, morbidly afraid of defeat. He prefers to be a spectator rather than a participant unless he is drunk and daft with Scotch courage. Scots are kidding themselves on when they think they are a sporting people. In fantasy the Scot might box with Lynch or Buchanan or Watt; he might run with Liddell and Wells; he might score goals with Denis Law and Dalglish; and might race with Jim Clark and Jackie Stewart. In fact the Scottish man in the street is the personification of unfitness. He screams for a Scottish victory from the terraces or, more suitably, from the boozer. His athletic heroes are vicariously projected as representative Scots though they are anything but. The typical Scot has bad teeth, a good chance of cancer, a liver under severe stress and a heart attack pending. He smokes like a chimney, drinks like a fish and regularly makes an exhibition of himself. He is a loser and he knows it. He is forever trying to cover up the pathological cracks in his character.

Secretly the Scot longs to be impressive, is dying to be a winner. The result is almost obscene. He expects to be battered into submission and readies himself for the challenge he is sure will come. He acts hard because the worst thing you can call him is a softie. The term has precise sexual connotations in Scotland. Way back the loss of Scottish independence, was experienced like a castration. To Scotsmen it meant a loss of independence, therefore a loss of manhood. Since 1707 at least, though the date defines an act rather than an attitude, the Scot has been trying to compensate for the agonising sense of loss by acting hard. Quite literally the Scot succumbs to a metaphor: he behaves like a walking weapon well aware of the phallic meaning of the word. In Scotland a man has to be seen to be hard. Hard as an erect weapon. Look at the urban hardman as he struts about the city. He does not walk: he surges forward. His motion is like the pumping of blood as he asserts his hard manhood. He is like a walking penis — a jock. A Scot is proud to be called a jock. He will say: we are all Jock Tamson's bairns.

Jock Tamson is the male organ. A jock is a penis personified. A jock has to be hard or he feels inadequate. A softie. In *The House with the Green Shutters* George Douglas Brown, a bastard who scarcely kent his faither, descibed the Scottish attitude towards the softie. 'To break a man's spirit,' Brown wrote, '(and) take that from him which he will never recover while he lives, send him slinking away *animo castrato* — for that is what it comes to — is a sinister outrage of the world. It is as bad as the rape of a woman, and ranks with the sin against the Holy Ghost — derives from it, indeed.'

To see the jock in action is to observe a spectacle capable of arousing pity for inside every hardman is a sensitive soul trying to escape. Yet escape is almost impossible for to be sensitive in Scotland is to be cissy — womanly — which is social death in a man's world where a man's man is a man for aa that. Scottish women have been treated with a mixture of terror and contempt in their twin roles as matriarch and mistress. John Knox, who acted to perfection the part of the Scottish hardman, put women firmly in their place in the celebrated first sentence of his 1558 manifesto *The First Blast of the Trumpet against the Monstrous Regiment of Women*. It reads: 'To promote a Woman to bear rule, superiorite, dominion, or empire above any Realme, Nation, or Citie, is repugnant to Nature; contumelie to God, a thing most contrarious to his reveled will and approved ordinance; and, finallie, it is the subversion of good Order, of all equitie and justice.' Knox was talking about queens in particular but in Scotland such sentiments have been applied to women in general. Thomas Carlyle was the most eminent of Scottish Victorians and widely thought of as a synonym for wisdom. When he was contemplating marriage to Jane Welsh he wrote to her at Haddington where, coincidentally, John Knox was born as Carlyle noted by planting an oak tree in honour of the Reformer. Carlyle's philosophy of marriage is contained in a letter sent to Jane in 1826: *'The Man should bear rule in the house and not the Woman.* This is an eternal axiom, the Law of Nature herself which no mortal departs from unpunished. I have meditated on this many long years, and every day it grows plainer to me: I must not and I cannot live in a house of which I am not head. I should be miserable myself, and make all about me miserable.'

The Scot — the typical Scot, the average Scottish writer — is marvellous at making all about him miserable. That is one of his grimmest duties, one taken very seriously indeed. He does not really believe that literature can alter the individual and yet that is the great quality of all art. Scottish writers *qua* typical Scots (and obviously I'm speaking for, and on behalf of, men here) are people who embody a destructive attitude to concepts like individuality and artistic integrity. Suspicious of everything they become failures but even these failures have flashes of the sensitive soul trying to get out.

A Glasgow Professor, G. Gregory Smith, in the course of an academic investigation into *Scottish Literature*, coined the phrase Caledonian Antisyzygy to account for 'the contrasts which the Scot shows at every turn, in his political and ecclesiastical history, in his polemical restlessness, in his adaptability . . . in his practical judgement.' More recently the psychiatrist, or antipsychiatrist, R.D. Laing used the phrase *The Divided Self* as the title of a study of the 'ontologically insecure person'. Laing is a Glasgow man born and bred and therefore well placed to come to conclusions about the nature of schizophrenia. He learned, in the city, what it means to be in the midst of an unfinished battle. Laing said, in *The Bird of Paradise,* 'We are shattered, tattered, demented remnants of a once-glorious army. Among us are Princes, and Captains of Armies, Lords of Battles, amnesic, aphasic, ataxic, jerkily trying to recall what was the battle the sounds of which still ring in our ears — is the battle still raging?' The question is rhetorical if the battle is Culloden when the clans were scattered, when Scottish pride was shattered, when the heroic Charles Edward Stuart turned out to be a loser — a Pretender — and so a very very Scottish figure. Laing's insight into the combat zone recalls the vision of a broken Scotland in Sir Walter Scott's first novel. As Edward Waverley moves through Scotland, after hearing of the defeat of the clans at Culloden, he sees clearly the consequences of conflict: 'As he advanced northward, the traces of war became visible. Broken carriages, dead horses, unroofed cottages, trees felled for palisades, and bridges destroyed or only partially repaired, — all indicated the movement of hostile armies.' There is internal evidence to suggest that the trauma Scotland suffered after Culloden was somewhat skin to the culture shock sustained by the Jews as a result of Nazi persecution.

Scotland is a divided and broken nation, the imperfect setting for Stevenson's Jekyll and Hyde, for Byron's Antithetical Mind, for Gregory Smith's Caledonian Antisyzygy, for R.D. Laing's Divided Self. Scotland presents its selves in counterpoint: Highland and Lowland, drunken and sober, Scots dialect and fake English, urban hard and sentimental soft, presbyterian and picturesque. There is a theory that this divisive nature might have ethnic origins. Julius Caesar thought so for he made an issue of it when writing about the Celtic peoples. 'The most remarkable feature about their political organisation,' he noted, 'is the existence everywhere of two great antagonistic parties. Not merely do these parties divide each independent tribe, but the cleavage extends to every territorial division and sub-division, and may almost be said to permeate every individual household.' That has a clear contemporary relevance. As the modern Scot is the result of a Celtic combination of Pictish and Irish elements them that heritage may have created disunity in the first place. Such indigenous tribalism could have flourished until it came to grief at Culloden when the clans were divided amongst themselves with tragic results. So the predicament of being a Scottish writer is a complex one just as the vicious literary gang has a precedent in the past and repercussions in the personality of the typical Scot today. I feel strongly, though, that it is possible for the Scottish writer to break the mould, to make himself entirely untypical by bringing out the creative individuality that lurks within him (a reverse of the process seen in *Dr Jekyll and Mr Hyde*). He will not do this by acting out pathological (hardman) fantasies, he will not do it by gathering in gangs. He will only do it by actually creating. Enough Scots have done this to make Scottish literature a great tradition and it is important to emphasise that the spirit of individuality has continued to materialise in print this century.

As long as the Scot conform to the pattern that has been thrust on him by a defeatist history he will be a washout whose nights before merge into endless mornings after. Yet he surely has a choice between being a typical Scot and becoming an individual. He can recreate himself in a wholly human image and throw off his subhuman trappings. In 1922 Christopher Murray Grieve, a postman's son from Langholm, recreated himself as Hugh MacDiarmid — a poet who was willing to make all the sacrifices necessary in order to save Scotland from itself. In 1926 he published *A Drunk Man Looks at the Thistle* which considers the mystery of the Scot and suggests a solution. The hero of the poem is, in the beginning, a typical Scot who staggers from the pub and wakes up on a hillside to see a thistle standing over him. It is a phallic symbol and an emblem of hope for as the drink wears off and the night recedes a new day comes and a new kind of consciousness dawns on the drunk man. He realises it is not enough to assert his Scottishness. He is, by an accident of birth, rooted in the reality of Scotland and sees that as both a blessing and a burden. He accepts his nationhood but at the same time reaches out towards the universe. The thistle is the weapon he uses to create a visionary unity that penetrates the universe. He is married to a woman and a sense of the past but wants more for he says:

> He's no a man ava',
> And lacks a proper pride,
> Gin less than a' the warld
> Can ser' him for a bride!

It is the contention of MacDiarmid's poem that the thistle can penetrate deep space, shoot out seeds like stars into the cosmos, and create a vision of the Scot as a spiritual being not an immature oaf dependent on spirit, on the hard stuff, the hard man's poison, or on hardmannerisms. This is the end of the predicament. The Scot can bring together all the elements that divide him. He can transform himself by an act of the imagination, can rise to a new sense of purpose. As the Drunk Man asserts his unique individuality he sees Scotland reborn:

> The thistle rises and forever will,
> Getherin' the generations under't.
> This is the monument o' a' they were,
> And a' they hoped and wondered.

The Scot has to become himself by becoming one with the unholy trinity of past, present and (especially) futures.

Such thoughts on the predicament of the Scottish writer come to me the week after my fortieth birthday when, proverbially, life begins. So be it. I hope this finds you well.

Alan Bold

ALAN RIACH
AFTER 300 YEARS

When they split, after three hundred years,
a strange thing happened, something
almost everyone hadn't expected:
the Northern mass began to move out to sea
with an inexorably ponderous consistency, and
a speed which seemed weightless, though great power
was in it; while the Southern mass, sinking slowly into sea,
slipped further South, and hitting the French coast,
was scuppered and went down, South first.
Meanwhile the North had gone,
amidst the European furore, and disappeared,
the hardy but scattered individuals
finding themselves as usual in a cold and
inhospitable place, suddenly much darker
than before, but somehow more curious, and more
demanding. Many died. In the great storms
and hurricanes, many were swept off the edge
and into a black void (and no-one knows where
they went) but those who remained
always had their hair blown by wind
their clothes soaked by rain, and their buildings
their cities and their villages, their fields
and mountains, stormed and pillaged by weather.
        From Europe a mild curiosity was affected
over the total disappearance of the Northern mass
from aerial photographs and tracking stations:
where could it have gone? By special instruments it was made certain
that it had not sunk like the Southern mass,
so they did not send out refugee troops.
The more curious expressed
a kind of wonder, that a land mass (even
so diminutive and inconsiderable a land mass)
should vanish. But it had. And sadly,
perhaps, after the extermination of the African peoples
and the explosion of India, the craterization
of central Asia and the eventual demise of China,
all the rest of the world got on very well,
until it died too. And then only the Northern mass,
somewhere in the outer darkness (or indeed
the inner) was left, whizzing through the
universe or perhaps not.

ALASDAIR GRAY

A MODEST PROPOSAL FOR BY-PASSING A PREDICAMENT

Last November the Edinburgh university press, Polygon Books, held a conference in the bar of the Traverse theatre club to publicise their reprint of Edwin Muir's book of the thirties, *Scott and Scotland*. The theme of the conference was The Predicament Of The Scottish Writer. On the platform were Iain Crichton Smith and myself and Trevor Royle and Alan Spence. Allan Massie was chairman. I had accepted his invitation to speak as immediately as a dog shuts its jaws on a proffered bone. Talking in public for a fee is much easier than writing sentences of informative prose, unless the talker writes the speech beforehand. It had not occured to me to do that. I had decided to be spontaneous yet modest. In referring to The Scottish Writer I would make no references to myself, so that the writers and students and theatre people and arts administration people in the audience would know I was speaking for all of them, too. And when I came to The Predicament I would ignore sexual, parental, educational, religious and emotional predicaments, since these vary from person to person. I would stick to poverty and unemployment, of which everyone has, or pretends to have had, considerable experience. In general terms I would explain that The Predicament Of The Scottish Writer is the predicament of the crofter and steelworker — the predicament of Scotland itself. What a radical, hardhitting yet humane speech that would be! Since there would be no crofters and steelworkers in the audience I would not upset a single soul.

I was first speaker and with a sinking heart saw Tom Leonard in the front row before me. He has a sharp ear for the glibly phony phrase. However, I managed to forget him, and with vehemence and quirkiness I delivered a speech so essentially bland that I cannot now remember a word I said. Then Iain Crichton Smith spoke sadly about the predicament of writing within, and for, the Gaelic and Lowland Scots language groups; and Trevor Royle spoke embarrassedly about the embarrassment of being born in England before writing in and about this place; and Alan Spence, in his soft, quiet, clear, hypnotic, evenpaced, level, voice, spoke in terms which were probably as general as my own, for I cannot now remember a word he said, either. Then Allan Massie, who had introduced us with the crisp firmness of a Victorian headmaster, invited questions and comment from the audience.

George Byatt asked why there were no playwrights on the platform. Did the conference organizers think writers for stage and television were negligible? Allan Massie replied that the conference has been organized by book publishers to publicise a book. Several other people made clear and necessary statements which led to no debate or exchange of ideas, because once uttered they seemed obvious. Eventually a troublemaker tried to get a positive expression of personal prejudice from the platform. He asked why there were no women on it. The chairman said nothing. The questioner asked the other speakers to comment on this and only I was stupid enough to do so. Forgetting that Joan Lingard was in the audience and that she and Muriel Spark and Jessie Kesson and Naomi Mitchison and Ena Lamont Stewart and Elspeth Davie and Ann Smith and Agnes Owens and Marcella Evaristi and Liz Lochhead would constitute a brace of quintets twice as dazzling as our enplatformed one, I stammeringly suggested that the proportion of male to female Scottish writers, statistically calculated, might, er, not, er, perhaps justify, er, the presence of more than half a woman ... Like a true friend Tom Leonard interrupted me here. He asked if this did not demonstrate that Scottish writing had basically homo-erotic foundation? I was able to change the subject by denouncing him for exposing our secret. Whereupon headmaster dismissed the entire class.

So I cannot remember the conference with much pleasure or interest, apart from an extract from Edwin Muir's *Scott and Scotland* which Allan read out at the start as an indication of what The Scottish Writer's Predicament was. Iain Crichton Smith took account of it at the time. I fudged it over. A few weeks ago I was answering a questionnaire sent by research students, and one of the replies became the speech I would have given at the conference if I had been honest enough to write it properly beforehand.

Q. An important consideration for any writer is the audience he wishes to reach; do you write for a Scottish audience primarily, or for a British audience or international audience? And do you feel that awareness of a potential readership in any way determines what and how you write?

A. I do not agree that an important consideration for *any* writer is the audience he wishes to reach. Writers who seek to persuade a limited class — commercial writers and propagandists — must think in that way, but I am sure that the stories and poems which the world has not yet allowed to die were written by folk who believed any ordinarily educated, sensible soul would enjoy them if they skilfully uttered what they thought important. I want to be read by an English-speaking tribe which extends to Capetown in the South, Bengal in the East, California in the West, and George MacKay Brown in the North. This does not preclude me from using any words of Scots origin that I please — dunt, docken, eerie, glamour, canny etcetera, or bunnet, polis, ya prickye, if I feel like being Glaswegian. The Indians have also given words to the English language, though at the moment only shampoo comes to mind. I am sure that Oxford and Cambridge have contributed useful words to the English language, though at present I cannot remember any. Most English words were originally used by illiterate Celts, Germans and Scandinavians. To these an international civil-service of priests added some long Latin words and a clan of bullyboy Norman invaders some posh French ones. In the past century the main additions to our vocabulary have been devised by scientists and technicians. Words stay alive because we find them useful or entertaining. An element in entertainment is surprise. One of the riches of English is the chance it gives to surprise the reader by putting a plain simple noun or verb, sometimes a strongly local one, into an abstractly posh-sounding sentence, and vice-versa. When a writer is using English dramatically — not necessarily in a play, it can be in a story where several speakers are quoted — the verbal colouring (if his characters are not bound to one social class in one emotional state) will be tinted with idioms which vary from biblical to the Johnsonian, from American film-commercial to local cockney, Oxbridge or Glaswegian. And this is simple realism. Any writers in English — if their range of reading is sufficiently wide — can take an exciting but generally unfamiliar word heard in a nearby street and, if it is useful, make the meaning and nuance plain to a reader from a different English idiom through the context in which it is marshalled. They can also use the prevailing diction of their locality, and if the thought and feeling is sufficiently strong and well expressed folk from other places who like good writing will teach themselves to understand. Burns demonstrated this two centuries ago. English literature took to him at once — if by Eng. Lit. we mean the acclaim of his fellow poets and every really intelligent reader. Scott and Hogg and Galt came soon after. Edwin Muir's frequently quoted formulation of the Scots writer's predicament into a double-bind choice of, write Scottishly and you'll be sincere but neglected by the world-as-a-whole, write for the English world-as-a-whole and you must discount the source of your emotions — seems to me nothing but a huge failure of nerve, a cowardice in the face of our best examples. MacDiarmid was one such example. He spoke of all the things he believed, using all the language he could master: local and historical, scientific-technical, political-polemical. One literary idiom was outwith his ken — the dramatic. Burns, Scott, Hogg, Galt could dramatize, find language for, people they were not. MacDiarmid had to make poetry from the dialectics of his self-contradictory intelligence. But that intelligence, that poetry, is still big enough for us to have worthwhile adventures inside. It is very queer that a small nation which has bred so many strongly local writers of worldwide scope still bickers and agonizes over the phony old *local versus international* doublebind. Why? The fact that Scotland is governed from outside itself, governed against the advice of the three Parliamentary Commissions and against the wishes of most Scots who voted on the matter, cannot be used to explain our lack of talent bacause that lack is no longer evident. Scotland has as many first rate writers as the USA had when Twain wrote *Huckleberry Finn* and a far greater crop of good second-raters, all surveying the universe across a Scottish foreground from the current of their particular Mississippi. There is no evidence that the local experience of Royal Home Counties writers gives them worthier subject matter or more intelligent dictions. Why should it? Does the proximity of a thing called a government inspire a finer class of thought? It might, if the government was fostering peaceful employment and social equality. It doesn't, so all it fosters is the wealth of the rich and a false sense of self-importance. John Braine feels more significant because Michael Foot nods to him in a restaurant, but the best London-based writers show lives as unblessed by government as Scotland is.

The foregoing diatribe is too long an answer to a short question. The short answer is, that since I resemble other people I can entertain and inform them if I entertain and inform myself with matter and language which do it best. This is a partial truth, but saves wasting time on market-surveys and public-relations work.

Alasdair Gray

JOHN HERDMAN

MUIR, SCOTLAND, DRINK AND FREE-WILL

When I first read Edwin Muir's *Scott and Scotland* some sixteen years ago I concluded that it was the most intellectually dishonest book by a distinguished mind that I had yet encountered. Perusal of this new edition does not, as I thought it might, expose that judgment as a mere reflection of the rash arrogance of callow youth; on the contrary, the conclusion does not come close to being disturbed by anything that I have read during the intervening swathe of time.

That the work is a polemical one is as good as admitted by Muir in his introductory chapter: Scott is being used as an occasion for an assault on Hugh MacDiarmid and the use of Scots as a medium for the composition of modern Scottish poetry. The dishonesty does not however lie in that all-but-declared intention, but in the nature of the procedures of argument which Muir adopts. The contention is made at the outset that there is a 'very curious emptiness' behind 'the wealth of (Scott's) imagination', and that this 'blemish' cannot be accounted for by any 'defect in Scott's mind and character'. Why not? Because 'men of Scott's enormous genius have rarely Scott's faults; they may have others but not these particular ones'. (Try arguing with that!) Muir is therefore 'forced' to seek the pathogenesis of this blemish in Scott's cultural situation. When, late and cursorily, he comes to consider Scott's case, he vouchsafes scarcely a gesture towards the principle that before a hypothesis can be considered proved, alternative explanations for the facts which it seeks to account for must first have been carefully examined and rejected. Instead, he first erects a monolithic structure of argument upon a selective reading of Scottish *poetry* (which he tacitly equates with literature in general), the upshot of which is the conclusion that since the sixteenth century Scotland has not been an 'organic community' possessing a 'homogeneous language' and hence is incapable of supporting an 'autonomous literature'. (The existence of MacDiarmid's 'remarkable' poetry in Scots is not for a moment permitted to dent the colossal assurance of Muir's cultural determinism: it is mentioned only to prompt the observation that 'he has left Scottish verse very much where it was before'.) The above conclusions, drawn from the evidence supplied by poetry, are then blandly applied to Scott's completely different cultural and linguistic situation as a prose writer, and used to explain the defects which Muir detects in his achievement as a novelist. But why, one might ask, use such an inapposite case as Scott's to make the point? Simple answer: Muir had been asked to write a book about Scott.

Allan Massie's introduction to the present edition, while it assesses the book's contribution to Scottish cultural debate considerably more generously than I could find it in my heart to do, most illuminatingly places a finger on many of the abounding inadequacies and distortions in Muir's specious argumentation. He suggests in particular (without quite saying as much) how style becomes an instrument of deceit: 'Muir's very cogent lucidity does lead him to simplify things excessively, to omit what is jagged or disruptive to his argument. It encourages him to use terms which he never properly defines, but which have a pleasing ring ... ' and it 'may lead him to distort his argument, for lucidity is often the result of a narrow vision'. The truth is that Muir specialises in setting up false dichotomies, formulated as epigrammatic but finally simplistic seeming-cogencies: the proposition that Scots think in one language and feel in another is but the most central and notorious of these. Certainly there is an attractive element of truth in this and certain other of Muir's formulations, but an element not nearly large enough to support the monolithic edifice which he raises upon them. Massie also convincingly demonstrates Muir's dependence on T.S. Eliot's literary criticism: the Scot makes use of Eliot's ideas and simulates his sentence structure and his Olympian tone while displaying none of his intellectual rigour.

In his concluding chapter, in rejecting Scots dialect poetry, Muir asserts that 'while we cling to it we shall never be able to express the central reality of Scotland, as Mr. Yeats has expressed the central reality of Ireland'. The sense of unity upon which the maintenance of national identity depends 'can be preserved', he says, 'by an act of faith, as it was in Ireland. Our task is to discover how this can be done; and I have tried to show how important the possession of a homogeneous language is for that end.' Since Muir nowhere in the book gives so much as an indication that he is aware of the existence of the Gaelic language, one might suppose that what he means is 'Write in English as I do, and all will be well.' Unfortunately, however, he has already ruled out the possibility of English being a 'homogeneous language' for the Scottish writer, since his definition of such a language is that the writer must be able both to think and to feel in it, and the Scots, he maintains, can think in English but *not* feel. This handicap, we must assume, accounts for Muir's failure to do for Scotland what Yeats did for Ireland.

Scott and Scotland is in reality as far removed as anything could be from an 'act of faith'. For all its elegance and superficial persuasiveness, for all its seeming concern for and engagement with Scotland's cultural plight, the attitude which it expresses is essentially that of a sad and mean-spirited defeatism; an attitude moreover which is adopted with a certain air of perverse and intransigent, if strikingly urbane, stubbornness. It is interesting today not for any positive contribution which it makes to the business of solving Scotland's cultural problems, but for the way in which its feeble but obdurate determinism furnishes an example of the very spiritual disease which it diagnoses.

The diagnosis is in places very sharp. The best passage in the book, it seems to me, is that in which Muir challenges Gregory Smith's view that Scots fantastic poetry reflects the capacity of the Scot to be at home as much in the invisible or supernatural as in the visible or natural world: ' ... Scottish fantastic poetry seems to me not to touch the second room of life at all; it is a pure escape, a pure holiday, whose ruling spirit is a Protestant Pope of Unreason.' In poetry like 'Tam O' Shanter' or Dunbar's 'Dance of the Seven Deidly Sinnis', Muir suggests, we are in a 'half-way-house', a 'mean altitude' between heaven and earth: 'It is a spirited recoil from the earthly which does not take one into too inconvenient proximity to the heavenly.' The part often played by drink in assisting the protagonist to such a position is particularly interesting, for drink was and is the classic image, and too often the medium, of Scottish spiritual defeatism. 'Finally,' says Muir, 'the drag of ordinary gravity pulls him back to earth again, and to explanations which satisfy the ordinary man, drink being the most natural of these. 'Tam O' Shanter' belongs to this kind of poetry, for drink is its principle as well as its imaginative explanation.' (The same, he might have added, is true of 'A Drunk Man Looks at the Thistle', at least as to its poetic framework.) Muir argues convincingly that imaginative intoxication of this kind is essentially an attempt to free oneself from the pressure of life, as such an expression of 'pure dissociation', and therefore finally 'a flouting of things in general, of Heaven and Earth and Hell, of God and Man, of the universal frame itself.'

In November last year, in connection with the republication of *Scott and Scotland*, a symposium was held in the Traverse Theatre, Edinburgh, on 'The Predicament of the Scottish Writer' (the sub-title of Muir's book). Five Scottish writers were invited to say what they felt their predicament to be, but worthily though they laboured the evening began to have a tired and jaded feel to it. The contributions from the platform took up a lot of time, but finally the discussion was thrown open to the floor, and a fairly lively though not very productive debate ensued. After about ten minutes, however, the chairman brought the meeting to a close. When I asked him later why he had curtailed the proceedings at this point, he replied that he had felt that everyone needed a drink; and until I began to think about it, this seemed to me to be a reasonable enough explanation. For we are quite accustomed in Scotland to regard drink as an unanswerable determinant, a need which must take precedence over all other considerations, an imperative before which one is powerless. Nothing must be allowed to get in the way of the demand for a drink, and one is, of course, quite helpless in the face of this overriding need. Such feebleness would in most contexts be regarded as contemptible, but in Scotland to challenge the position of drink as a consideration to which priority must unfailingly be granted appears, if not unmanly, at least anti-life.

The role of drink in Scottish life as a prop, an excuse and an explanation is a true manifestation of spiritual and moral weakness, and the way it functions in these regards is faithfully reflected in Scottish literature. Drink furnishes a ready and supposedly unanswerable excuse for anything reprehensible done under its influence: 'I was pissed when I done that'; 'Mr. N. MacKay, defending, explained that at the time of the offence Dignan had been drinking.' The *locus classicus* for this is of course in 'Holy Willie's Prayer':

> Besides, I farther maun avow,
> Wi' Leezie's lass, three times — I trow —
> But, Lord, that Friday I was fou
> When I cam near her:
> Or else, thou kens, thy servant true
> Wad never steer her.

If, on the other hand, the experience of drink gives rise to anything positive, to anything serious, to anything spiritually valuable, as at times indeed it can, then its provenance in drink will be used to undercut it and devalue it, cut it down to size. The *locus classicus* for this is the conclusion of 'A Drunk Man Looks at the Thistle':

> O I ha'e Silence left,
>
>
>
> — 'And weel ye micht,'
> Sae Jean'll say, 'efter sic a nicht!'

Is Jean's voice here the expression of reliable, down-to-earth realism, the earthy side of the Caledonian antisyzygy, as it is usually taken to be? Or does it rather speak in the cynical, reductive idiom that mocks immaterial truths, that seeks to explain and domesticate them, to accommodate them to fit one's own smallness of soul?

Muir relates to the cultural condition of Scotland very much as so many of his countrymen relate to the phenomenon of drink which somehow so aptly symbolises it — as something that can't be resisted and must be bowed down to, something before which our free-will is in abeyance, something that excuses our failures but at the same time devalues our achievements. It is perhaps not so surprising, then, that when Scottish writers gather to face their predicament the first true response to assert itself is the need to have another drink. Yet Allan Massie makes a vital point when he contends, against Muir, 'Yet it is the case that Writing also exists as Freedom. The writer can choose, as MacDiarmid chose; and any successful outcome, however partial, itself becomes part of the tradition the next generation inherits.' If the Scottish psychic knot manifests itself as repeated failure of whole-hearted commitment — which was just what happened in 1979 — that failure can indeed be seen as one of collective will; but is collective will really anything other than the coming-together and co-operation of individual wills? Muir sees the problem as being one 'for the Scottish people as a whole, not for the individual Scottish writer; for only a people can create a literature.' In some rarified and ethereal sense this is no doubt true, but there is also an obvious sense in which it *is* individual writers who create a literature, and so long as Scottish writers continue to project their failure onto 'the people', or their collective cultural situation, they will continue to have a scapegoat to hand nearly as useful as drink to excuse that failure. If, as an individual Scottish writer, I fail to do what I hope to do and potentially am capable of doing, I had better come quickly to terms with the fact that the fault is finally my own; and endless girning about the collective 'predicament' is unlikely to be conducive to this insight.

The Scottish people, writers included, have perhaps been too long intimidated by the God without to listen heedfully to the voice of the God within, with whom all things are possible. Yet that voice has not seldom been heard in the course of Scottish literature. The spirit I am thinking of is nowhere more simply and directly expressed than in the closing words of Fionn MacColla's *Scottish Noël*, when the defeated Scottish army is regrouping and setting off in the night to face the enemy once more and fight another day:

Voices of gruff command, clinking of arms, hoof-beats and foot-falls, all the opaque grey-pallid snow-filled night ... following, ever-following south. Christ in the will, the blow befallen earlier was nothing ... not even a feather.

John Herdman

Note: *Scott and Scotland,* by Edwin Muir, is published by Polygon Books, 114pp., £5.95. *Scottish Noël* by Fionn MacColla is available, price £1.50 from Mary MacDonald, 51, Warrender Park Road, Edinburgh, as is *'At the Sign of the Clenched Fist'* by the same author.

ALAN RIACH

NORTH

The fishes' sightless eyes, drowning,
Cast back upon cold waves
(—The cranners would not have them—)
Whirl the stony world around them,
Like a revolving stone axe,
Swinging like a great fowl caught up in a storm,
All flesh and seed
And pebbles like round, hard eggs,
Making a circle like Scotland's sound.

Hard and swift and sharp,
The red knife's silver blade
Halves mackerel on a plate glittering with scales.
The knuckles gutting wedge and grate.

The sculling fleeing claws,
Wound on the flesh of the angled god,
The Osprey, taut strength beating,
Wings over bare spears of stalks
Waving on a crofter's site.

—Scotland is surrounded on all sides with sea,
Except one, to which it bears
A proximity much like a candle
Burning brightly in the black eye-socket
Of a tremendous skull.

WILLIAM NEILL

FETCH ONY NATIVE SCOTTISH BIRD.

Fhionnlaidh Mac Dhonnachaidh Dhuibh Mac Phaidein
c'àite a bheil an gille wi the poc breac,
Is mòr an aire takin trewis breikless mac braidean ...

These are the first three lines of a macaronic poem by Alexander Montgomerie (c.1500) who was a son of Montgomerie of Hazelhead in Ayrshire. The poem is partly in Gaelic, partly in Scots, since southern Ayrshire at that time was solidly Gaelic speaking; Montgomerie's bilingualism is unremarkable to modern Gaelic scholars although it is still a matter of jaw-hanging disbelief among many so-called 'educated Scots'. Although the Gaelic in the version above is in the orthodox Scottish spelling of that language, Montgomerie in his own version used the orthography of *Scots,* which led many foolish people in former days to think he was writing gibberish. Other Scottish bilingual men of letters such as Holland *(The Book of the Howlat)* and the MacGregor family of Fortingall *(The Book of the Dean of Lismore)* used the same system. They are, nevertheless, writing in perfectly good Gaelic. At the recent Celtic Chair Centenary meeting in the University of Edinburgh Dr. Donald Meek gave a skilful elucidation of these Gaelic/Scots poems. The verses and their orthography give the lie to asses who claim that Gaelic was never spoken south of the Forth-Clyde line or east of the Grampians, and the equally egregious donkeys who assert that no Highlander ever spoke Scots but resorted to the pristine Laura-Norder dialects of the Cockney south whenever he might be obliged to abandon Gaelic.

Within countries where different languages dwell in close proximity, macaronic poems are common; poets, after all, like to play with words. MacDiarmid was fond of the macaronic game, sometimes on a level of high seriousness.

Muscail do mhisneach a Alba
Set up your *Cuirt na h-eigse*
with a resounding *Barrantas,* my friends.

therein expressing a hope that 'Scottish' writers might at least try to be Scottish. It also shows a considerable knowledge of the literary tradition common to Ireland and Scotland, touching as it does on a literary activity which flourished under oppression.

There is no doubt in anyone's mind that the writers mentioned above were *Scottish* writers, for their languages show them to have been such. Using a Scottish language in whole or in part is one way of putting a Scottish stamp on writing. Had Hume left his work with the original Scotticisms uncorrected he just might have been known as the great Scottish philosopher, which he was, rather than by his more frequent epithet of the great *English* philosopher, which he certainly was not.

Any article on Scottish literature must be heavily weighted towards an examination of the qualifying adjective. It must be borne in mind that it is *Scottish* writing that concerns us and not *British* writing by Scots or others living within Scotland. It is, of course possible for non-Scots living in Scotland to produce distinctly Scottish writing if they absorb enough Scottishness through the soles of their feet, so to speak. The Great Scottish Language problem is always there facing us, and is not to be abondoned for a limp surrender to standard southern English, or standard southern English attitudes.

Whatever language a person chooses to write in is no business of mine until the claim is made that the writing is *Scottish;* then the choice of language becomes my business too. As a reader I am entitled to agree or disagree as to whether a piece of work so described merits its title, or whether it should be described as English or British. I dislike the latter term as it properly describes a group of Cymric tribes rather than a literary ambit, but there is no help for it. Mere geography will not solve the problem. Miss Beckwith's mock-Gaelic extravaganzas may be set in the Gaidhealtachd and may well be written there; no one with the slightest perception would call these productions 'Scottish'. They are, in fact, thoroughly English; the inner Sasunnach shines through so that the Scots she paints are a sort of quaint non-existent garden-gnome-type-Gael acceptable in the remote South. On the other hand, Clifford Hanley's *A Taste of Too Much* must be instantly seen as Scottish to anyone who has been an adolescent in an urban Scottish environment. We know his characters because we have met most of them in real life, in our own country. Think of the Irishman Joyce sharing the journey of an ancient Greek adventurer and setting it down in Paris, unable to escape from his Irishness. He is writing in English, but Anier Mac Con Glinne, maker of satires, is sitting at his elbow.

In the same way a novel written in English is not necessarily un-Scottish, but its Scottishness depends on the inner Scottishness of the writer shining through the language. Of course, if your aim is to cater to London parochialism do not allow this to happen except at the most Caledonian Garden-Gnome level. Writing in English which rings true in any Scottish way will probably not be appreciated by London critics commuting nightly to the flat holms and quiet downs of the Home Counties. The horny-handed earthiness of Grassic Gibbon's Angus did not travel well when it was shown on their local telly. It was Gibbon's inner Scottishness that was too much for them. Now I am not saying that the English ought to admire genuine inner Scottishness if they prefer tartan gnomes; but *Scots* ought to prefer it if they claim to be *Scottish* writers. Otherwise they ought to emigrate to a more congenial mental climate and write there.

Speaking personally, I prefer what is written in our more native tongues, although I am aware that in the thin air of the present Scottish Parnassus this is looked on as eccentric. Most of the really good stuff in our older tongues is poetry although good prose has been increased in quantity during the past twenty five years, both in Gaelic and Scots. Poetry has a stronger hold over Scottish minds that any other art form. I am talking here about poetry at all levels, from folk-song to bardic eulogy. Nowadays Gaelic and Scots are caviare to the general: and that general includes all but a very small caucus of publishers. Difficult as it is to get Scots and Gaelic into print, a courageous group still manages to produce, in fair numbers, books of Scottish writing in our native languages. This is especially true of Gaelic. To my mind (and I am a man of the south-west) the best literature (Scottish!) is that written in Gaelic. While MacDiarmid was alive there were doubts as to who led the field; now there is none. Gaelic leads the field in my opinion, not only in poetry but in prose, for *Gairm Publications, Acair,* and *Club Leabhar* have brought out a deal of good prose by eminent writers as well as poetry. It is a great pity that the short stories of, say, Iain Crichton Smith, in Gaelic, do not have the readership that he has in English. I cannot see why it should seem so difficult for Scots to be cultured in the fascinating three-stranded way that is the legacy of our history. After all, MacDiarmid was, and all the Scottish literati must agree that he must be taken seriously. For example:

> But, och, when I cam
> To Arts and Letters
> The gomerils gapit
> And shamed their begetters!
> Even Muireadach Albannach,
> Lachlan Mòr of his stem,
> And Finlay MacNab
> Meant nothing to them!

These deceptively simple lines are an extremely skilful production. This verse is in three languages. Firstly he shows the viability of modern Scots by introducing a few words still in use. But he weaves this Scots strand into a verse containing *deliberate* standard English. Had he intended it to be solidly Scots he would have found a way to change the fourth line into Scots ... for example *schamit* rather than *shamed*; and *tae* rather than *to, naething* for *nothing*. He then tacks on three eminent poets to give the verse a Gaelic flavour, as well as to make his point to such Scots as are literate enough in their own culture to pick it up. This is the main strand of the rope on which he intends to hang the ignorant anglicisers of the Scottish educational system, particulary in the four ancient universities. He demonstrates that he is not ignorant of the Scottish Gaelic connection with the background of common classical poetry in that tongue in both Scotland and Ireland, for Muireadach Albannach (Scotch Murray) is that descendant of the Bardic family of the O Dalaigh, who fled to Scotland in the thirteenth century and founded the Scottish line of MacMhuirich bards. MacDiarmid feels this heritage in his bones and knows that he shares in it. At any rate he certainly took Finlay MacNab's advice:

> *Sgriobh gu fiosach fireòlach*
> *a seanchas is a gcaithreim ...*

'Write knowledgeably and with true learning of their history and song'. It is quite possible, as MacDiarmid shows, to capture the Gaelic aspect of our culture (common to 'Lowland' as well as 'Highland' Scotland; up to 1380 there was no dichotomy) but as he so succinctly points out this requires *literary* learning of the Scottish background. Not the naive historical-romance rubbish which blows around the conceited harn-pans of many who style themselves *Scottish* writers, but a true awareness of the rich Scottish background. Even the English have an awareness that Arthurian tales, Gawaine and the Green Knight, Tristan and Isolde are figures from *Celtic* sources; educated and even *literary* (!!) Scots often do not know the name of their own country in the first Scottish language. Scottish culture is to be seen in its depth and breadth by all who would aspire to the epithet *Scottish* in the field of writing, and a mere 'Scottish' extension to First Ordinary Eng. Lit. without any reference to the Gaelic background is not enough.

Gaelic requires no index other than itself to show its Scottishness. There can be few, even among what I call the London-Scottish school of writers (trimmers of their work to suit London publishers) who have not heard of the poets whose work is contained in the recently published *Nua-Bhardachd Ghaidhlig (Southside):* Sorley MacLean, George Campbell Hay, Iain Crichton Smith, Derick Thomson and Donald MacAulay. Some idea of their excellence can be got from reading the translations supplied. All of those poets have individual collections, mostly with English translations, and ought to be read by any claimant to the title of *Scottish* writer. But there is also a younger generation of excellent poets to follow on. Gaelic literature is *not* going to die out to suit the wishes of the one-language fanatics, and the fact that there are intelligent Gaelic-speaking children growing up in Scotland today will ensure its influence into the next century at least.

In the last issue of *Chapman* I read Aonghas MacNeacail's words:

> *gu'n mhiannaich mi*
> *an leine chroic, ...*

MacNeacail desires the saffron cloak worn by men of rank amongst the Gael of old. This is the cloak which would also have been worn by poets, since in those enlightened days poets were considered to be men of rank by virtue of their art. The Gaelic Ayrshireman Walter Kennedy was accused by Dunbar of wearing such a garment; Dunbar, an anglophile in the great Scottish southward-looking tradition, did not like this evidence of Gaelic-ness on Kennedy's part. Any man who wore the *leine-chroic* would be versed in our own past history and tradition. Except for a few bright figures here and there I do not see many of those who currently sit on literary platforms as 'Scottish' writers, who deserve, figuratively speaking, to wear the *leine-chroic,* since most of them seem to be breaking their necks to inherit John Bull's waistcoat of southern acceptability. You may, of course, deliberately abandon Scottishness altogether, but then you should not pose on public platforms as a *Scottish* writer. North British is the name for *you.* What a *Scottish* writer needs is not so much a public face as a functioning backbone.

You can easily test whether you are likely to qualify for the metaphorical *leine-chroic* of present day literary Scotland. If you have an intense and ever-present feeling that you are a member of a culture under siege then your Scottishness is probably intact.

One of the favourite tactics of the southward-seeking school of 'Scottish' literati is to accuse those who stick to Scots, Gaelic, or even Scottish attitudes in Standard English, of being backward-looking. Looking backwards is something which happens to cultures that are under attack; the defenders tend to become, to a certain extent, *laudatores temporis acti.* To my mind this is as valid a literary stance as any other provided it is controlled; it is certainly a truer index of native feeling than the pseudo-progressive babblings of the fakes, and it is surely conceivable that some aspects of past times *were* better than the present, unless your conceptions are hampered by some constraining philosophy or other.

Ruaraidh MacThomais (Derick Thomson already mentioned) writing of John MacLean in his poem *Armann* ends with these words:

> Iolach a' Ghaidheil
> a' tighinn a chliabh na Ghalldachd;
> nam biodh seasmhachd as a lasair
> sgriobhte 'Saorsa' air neamh Alba fhathast.

'The Gael's exultant cry/coming from the chest of the Lowlands;/if only the flame lasted/it would write 'Freedom' on Scotland's sky yet.'

Respice prospice. The best words in the best order expressing for me exactly what I feel about Scotland in general and Scottish writing in particular. **William Neill**

WILLIAM NEILL

SCOTIA EST DIVISA IN VOCES TRES. (A MACARONIC BALLAD)

Tonight I trauchled around on top of the hill
reflecting on what a stubborn *bodach*[1] I am
keeping thrissles and gowans alive in my memory still,
playing treason to God knows what international plan.

Linguistic rebellion should be written in Scots
or Gaelic or Glasgow glottals however broad;
but Scottis, wae's me, is smoort by their pan-loaf plots
an it's no the *luchd-na-Gaidhlig*[2] I ettle tae scaud.

But tonight this flyting came rattling into my head
in the fancy English they've taught me for years to speak;
and although my other two tongues are not quite dead,
yif I yaised ae leid or tither, *cha bhithinn glic*[3].

*Is nan robh mi a 'bruidhinn Gaidhlig tha fiòsam gle mhath
is e teuchter a chanadh iad rium 'san aineolais mòr:
cànain a shabhail Roinn-Eorpa 'san Dorchadas trath
'na cuspair am bial amaideach air son spòrs.*[4]

All over Alba Gaelic shouts from the stones
to those who have ears to hear, though there's Damn Few left
who can feel their heritage ache like rheumatic bones;
the rest, of all worthy sensations quite bereft

think, if they wave a Lion Flag in your eyes
or stab a synthetic haggis once a year
that this will provide an adequate disguise
for thairms and painches swilled completely clear

of almost anything worthy the native name.
They seem to be chained to shadows that dance in the cave,
(ten light-years away from their Grannie's Hielant Hame)
where they mutter over a mantra of Scotland the Grave.

Is it I who am mad because I will not abandon
the thorns and thistles that made me what I am?
To gain a southern approval or North-British standing
must I swap native spice for International Jam?

The true Scottish essence is none too hard to define
whether you think it a blessing or a blot;
In MacGill-eain and MacDiarmid you'll taste that wine
that runs bitter or sweet on the older tongues of the Scot.

Puir auld Dunbaur wi mortis conturbat intyre,
twas the mooth-pairchin Inglis that he thocht the mair parfyte;
he lights in my heart a much less comforting fire
than that which Walter Kennedy set alight . . .

when Gaelic, he said, should be all true Scotsmen's tongue,
that Scotland it caused to prosper and to spread;
now, ochanee, when our Scottishness is sung
a new tongue stands an old truth on its head.

I'm like a fish that's caught in a dowie doagh;
I wait with impatience and but a little hope
to feel in my gills the freedom of the loch
wherein my urge to swim will be given scope.

You don't even have to beat their forty-per-cent[5] . . .
all that you need is an ear kept to the ground
of the *siubhal, tuarluath, crunluath*[6] that was meant
to keep your gutstrings tuned to a Scottish sound.

ENVOI TO THE DEAN'S BOOK[7]

A man concerned greatly for old forms:
syllabic counts of predatory bards,
three hundred pages (quatro in gilded boards)
of ill-spelt Gaelic; a sheaf of leaves to catch
the spirit of a passing time; a clutch
anxiously placed under decorated wings
to hold the fading scent of passing things.

My dull edition, more the worse for wear
than any vellum; backed by scholar's notes;
comparison of varying recensions where
what the bard spoke may seem of less import
than learned surmise is, however short.
Vauntings, laments and stately homiletics
now share a page with variant phonetics.

A Gaelic link that is not mere sentiment
(evening class guide-book, tried on holiday
with bed and breakfast; clan society merriment,
brief patriotic toasts on St Andrew's day)
goes to the heart of Scotland in the one true way.
The black jewel of Aiffric's grief set against gold
remains until this hour as bright and cold.

Prisoned between two ages the good Dean tried
to crush this gathered crop into small case.
Red Finlay's rhymed excuses have not died;
The Bard MacLintock has not ceased to chase
profit by toadying to Duncan's race
in the best *Ae Freislighe* he could summon forth
hoping his skill might win for him a horse.

Now the last heirs turn from the Dean's work
setting their eyes to a baser store of wealth,
regard as madmen the true sons who lurk
under the shadow of a dusty shelf.
There, under that least illuminated edge
all that is truly Scottish is confined
far from what passes as the native mind.

NOTES: 1. Old man. 2. Gaelic speakers. 3. 'I would not be wise'. 4. 'And if I were to speak Gaelic I know well that they would call me a teuchter in their great ignorance . . . the language that saved Europe in the Dark Ages is a subject for sport in a foolish mouth'. 5. A reference to Mr. Cunningham's amendment. 6. Movements in The Great Music. 7. The Book of the Dean of Lismore: a collection of Scottish Bardic poetry compiled about 1530.

SABBATH WALK

Walking on the hill's the only thing worth while
after the Sunday papers; London style
journalism that tries to take the place
of vanished rituals, but lacks their grace.
It is not likely that the great will care
for old men's brooding over things long gone:
old faiths, old tongues, the runes we leaned upon.
Blackface sheep are the only audience here.

Wordsworth wandered under wheeling plovers,
boomed behind hedges and scared rural lovers;
he knew the ghost that lived in rock and thorn,
could not escape groves, being druid-born.
We do not have his audience to share
his cadences; start from his common ground
to sense the deeps that lie beneath the sound.
Where are they now who once had ears to hear?

Hard at work on an urban confrontation
at levels fitting to the rank and station
not to be seen here in this empty land:
sloping rigs with hawthorn on either hand.
In my lone head I bear antique reasons
for sky and water, rock and thorn and cloud,
the road that leads me from cradle to shroud;
flesh divided into seven seasons.

Each seven years they say a man's renewed
from head to toe. With what are we imbued
that holds our dying substances in one
from the first suck until the whole thing's done
and all our dust and moisture split and spread?
Some secret otherness than flesh and bone
that links the child to age when cells are gone:
the hidden matrix of the heart and head.

Alembic to electron microscope;
in all their science not a meagre hope
that they can formulate this unseen mist
which into our more solid flesh is pressed;
a shade no man-made gear can mark or trace;
a flash caught only in the mystic mind
when reason's calculation's left behind,
for there's no law or logic fits the case.

The ram that moves within the thicket there,
covers his mistress with no courtly air.
A mouth and bowel motion; oestrogen
dictates his lust; unlike the way of men
who of their procreation make a game
played out in joy or pain as fits the case
with no more eye towards the future race . . .
but give the ram's task a poetic name.

The beasts that move upon the hillside here
are moved by herd-life, hunger, lust and fear.
I wonder all cannot see man's clear case
lies beyond this poor gift in granted grace.
It is the moving spirit that makes man
the sole possessor of clear thought and choice,
arrangement, pattern, altruism's voice,
great art and memory and soul and plan.

In fleshly procreation egg and seed
march down the centuries to make the breed.
But we are bound by other, unseen chains,
for when the bone is dust, this wraith remains.
Today I walk in step with it on the hill;
the unseen footsteps of the other walkers
fill the grey Sabbath silence with their talking.
When I am coffined, I may walk here still.

For it is not mere flesh, the weight of bone
crushes this grass and stumbles on this stone,
but all things linked to one yet separate,
a one-not-one with a much greater state
in which upon this hill I join and part
as the mind fills and ebbs with every step;
by rock and root and drystone dyke and slap
the stillness of true knowledge fills the heart.

Now in still hope, down from the hill again,
back to the weary cities of the plain
that in their complications ape the beast,
make in their greatness, false gods of the least.
Traherne knew all about the Landlord's will;
the great lordship that stretches to the rim
of vision, or the reach of willing limb.
All that's worth while is walking on the hill.

William Neill

MARY CAMERON

ONE WOMAN OF LEWIS

Yesterday I did not see you old
and stooping
in the gentle kindly way
that time, unresented,
brings to those
who have not craved to see
revenge called justice,
or held themselves
to ransom, on their knees.

Yesterday you looked to claim
a Lewiswoman's role
and cast aside some vague unease
that made your island
slip the mesh

of maps and globes
and satellites;
that made the special
rather plain
and wooed your mind to wakefulness
with the soft sound of laughter.

For hours and years
and days,
that came and went,
and brought new thoughts,
new ways of love
and pain;
that spent
the old known vanity of youth.

Those days, in cliched trance,
have failed to fire
their meaning into words
but you who do,
and weep,
and smile,
I see have borne the faith
in Life itself.

AS THE ISLAND SLEEPS

As the island sleeps
she dreams
the far-off dreams of time and youth
and their echoes mingling with the sound of the tide
on Uig's beaches
and Seaforth's shores,
bring home to her her sons,
bring back the laughter,
the sediments of fun.

The island and her lover
have lived too long to leave the morning
to its own endeavour;
the bonds have long been sealed
and change absorbed
like rain on the marshes
and like the old dew of summer.

Some days and nights
when she listens,
the far-off cries of 'Lewis!' deceive her into thinking
than longing is hungered by distance
and returning an emigrant's dream.

Another turn and trick of time,
and another generation
grows up with the tired words of chorused songs,
sung louder on return visits home
and on ceilidh nights in Glasgow.

The island
and the moving sea,

people no longer poor enough to leave
seem a little too anxious to remain;
an island of croft and moor;
a still giant sea,
night-time gales,
windswept shores,
Gaelic and gentle slow voices
— and an outside world coming in with each dawn.

AUTUMN THOUGHTS
Evening of Peace
2nd October — my father died

Evening, a peaceful end to an October day,
the moors lie back
and sigh;
show their colours
of rust and fawn, blue to grey
and the hills hidden in the shadows
of timelessness and dusk.

Earth, red and brown and black,
that kindles time and us
to know more things.
Peat fires burning,
blue smoke to blue skies rising
gone for a while,
unseen, unheard.

Murmurings in the hollows
among the hills,
murmurings of memories
awakened by the peace,
lying softly awake
to let us feel
we shan't be biding long.

A touch of gold in the autumn sky
fading out like a stranded ember
of the fire,
boasting of the fleeting trances of time
— and God's control.

The wind is dead,
the night sky waits,
and cradling our fears
dare we wonder why?
Why a death
of one so dear —
Those miracles that stretch
to places
where we forget to look.

Evening in autumn
peace for the blessed
and time
drawing scenes
we don't recognise.

THE HUNT

Strange,
those hills that beckon
to the men who go hunting
with sighted rifles
and camouflage jackets
— to hunt
    and poach
    the deer forest stage.

Early day
rising white and silver behind the hills of Park
lightly strokes away
the shadows of the night;
doors quietly close,
haversacks are checked,
and the hunters fall in silent twos
to gauge their way
on unseen beaten tracks.

Their empty-bellied grandfathers knew the hunt,
and not for stage
or sport
their larking tales of a gamie's chase
begged a clever telling;
strange,
men's claims on the hills
to family life.

They follow sounds
the men of the hunt
that travel from time to a time long gone
when the venison was sweeter
and lighter to lift;
boys to men
and memories fade
but have failed to die.

Strange,
the hills that wait
for the men of the hunt,
and hold the deer,
full-fed,
sheltered in hollows,
protected by wind.
Cruel
the scent on the wind
of a man on the hunt
to the deer in the hills
whose stock
long since surrendered its best.

Mary Cameron

GEORGE KEREVAN

LABOURISM REVISITED

Scotland was never socialist. On the contrary, it has been dominated by Labourism, an anglo-centric, reformist creed developed in the working class wing of nineteenth century English liberalism. Labourist politics, including its Scots bastard off-spring, is based on caste rather than class; on seeking recognition for the claims of the untouchables within the eternal framework of specifically British society. What makes Labourism different from European socialism is that it has provided the central pillar of support for national integration. Toryism worked wonders on a narrow, chiefly English, middle class but it would never have been enough to hold together the most proletarian state in Europe. Labour is now in crisis precisely because its ideological rationale is disintegrating with the very society for which it provided the cultural cement. In effect, the British political crisis is the crisis of Labourism itself, and like sub-atomic particles loosed off from the decay of the old, the outcome of this crisis will determine the future of Scottish politics. British Labourism's difficulty is Scottish socialism's opportunity.

But to know the future we must first understand the past. The pivotal period in Twentieth century Scots history are the years 1915 to 1919, the one time when might have been born a genuine Scottish socialism aimed at eliminating class domination. Here occurred momentous events: the Glasgow rent strike, the anti-war agitation of MacLean and the general strike for the forty hour week. This wave of working class unrest ended in bitter defeat. In a striking parallel with events in the north of Italy — the Turin factory occupations of 1921 — the shop steward vanguard of the Scottish working class held social power in its hands but was unable to turn it into political power. MacLean's instinctively correct demand for working class political independence north of the border as an attempt to place power on the agenda was seriously weakened by his own sectarianism to the still reformist, but radicalising, mass of workers in the Labour Party: an ultra-leftism towards united fronts he shared with Silvia Pankhurst and a sizeable minority of the Communist International in Western Europe.

In the vacuum that followed defeat the leadership of the Scots workers' movement passed into the hands of reformist Labourism. Tangible reforms did appear — jobs for Catholics as well as Protestants, houses for all — but the unique element in the package was that because the revolutionary leadership had been broken the Labourists and Clydeside Capitalists could unite on a common programme to demand economic aid for Scottish industry from London. This supplicant strategy implied a New Unionist Consensus in place of the old Labour movement demand for Home Rule. Instead of Home Rule there was St. Andrews House, the Scottish Council (Development and Industry) and frequent junkets to London to discuss the prospects for more investment.

The co-option of the radical wing of the British working class into a grand Historic Compromise with Capital had repercussions outwith Scotland: it helped to strengthen Labourism in its task of marrying proletarian Frankenstein to English patrician society. Scotland paved the way for the displacement of reformist preoccupations from social welfare provisions to economic management, though another generation would pass before Keynes converted the English Establishment to this idea as a solution to national economic failure. The elitist, Eighteenth century state with its monarchy, House of Lords and anti-industrial bias was safe while Labour was mesmerised by economic tinkering. Labour left the Establishment and City bankers alone and created massive, bureaucratically-run nationalised monopolies as charity wards for a Capitalist class too decadent or incompetent to modernise.

In the late Sixties and early Seventies Scottish Labourism lost mass working-class support to the SNP through being unable to advance a positive solution to the incipient decay of British society. Only by tentatively re-embracing the old Home Rule demand with its subversive implications for the future of the geriatric British state was the SNP challenge fended off just in time. And after years of Thatcher even the anti-devolution wing of the Scottish Labour Party has acquiesced to the call for an Assembly with full economic powers. But has the leopard really changed its spots? Has the Unionist Consensus collapsed? Cynics can rest assured: deep down the Scottish Labour Party is undergoing a transition which will explode fortress Labourism.

Labourism's unique strength in Scotland rested on a particular network of alliances which are now decomposing: its use of intellectuals as an organic link with society, unlike England where they were mere 'programme writers'; its use of the Communist Party as its industrial arm; its hegemony over the dense concentration of industrial workers in the West of Scotland.

Firstly the intelligentsia: politically the English intelligentsia as a whole has been either co-opted into the state machine through the Civil Service, or exiled into academic Olympia at Oxbridge. The Labour Party's relationship with its English intellectuals, from the Webbs to Bernard Crick, has been to keep them in the display cabinet. They were for show, not for bringing out where they might contaminate politics with ideas. The British Labour Party's intellectuals talked to other intellectuals. But not so in Scotland.

The teachers and ministers who staff the Scots intelligentsia are from lower middle-class or upper working-class backgrounds rather than the high bourgeoisie of Hampstead. They are produced by a university system which, while only relatively democratic, is imbued with a tradition of turning out not just the ruling elite but the cadres who run all Scottish civil society. This classically Gramscian organic intelligentsia felt itself the genuine leadership of the popular masses and not a partrician intellectuals' closed shop. In the political realm the English archetype is Keynes: brilliant, arrogant, aloof, rich, from an academic family. In Scotland it is a MacLean or even a Reith, with a mission to educate rather than illuminate.

Scottish Labourism would neither have been created nor have survived as the dominant structure in Scots politics had it not used the local intelligentsia as its social cement. The ethos of 'service' and 'education' as well as the poor material position of those lower middle-class intellectuals propelled them into the Labour Party. From Maxton to Pollock to Ross, school teachers provided the intellectual fodder of Scots Labourism till the values of the party and the values of the educational system itself became inextricably bound up. Further, Labour's Catholic communalism in the West of Scotland ensured that Catholic intellectuals gravitated towards it, linking church and party. Marxist intellectuals joined the Communist Party, but in Scotland that was a mass CP which by dint of its social weight was accepted as an integral part of the Labour movement. A modus vivendi existed between Labour and Communist which brought CP intellectuals into the bosom of Labourism: witness Hamish Henderson or Ken Alexander. Finally, the national question itself played a role, for whether politically nationalist or not, Scots intellectuals felt themselves born of a different culture and this 'otherness' spawned a radicalism which fuelled support for the left among the entire intelligentsia.

Today the Scottish intelligentsia has defected from Labourism as a creed. In the Seventies and Eighties it has become overwhelmingly politically nationalist while retaining its old social radicalism. This resulted from a change in the composition and role of intellectuals in Scotland. The Sixties and early Seventies saw Scottish universities flooded with the sons and daughters of the working class, all imbued with the Labourist welfare state notion that education was a passport to the good life. This swollen mass of the new professional middle class rapidly became disenchanted with the realities of secondary school teaching in Drumchapel and Pilton. One side-effect was the wave of teachers' strikes throughout the Seventies, a telling break with the service ethos. The most significant result, however, has been the explosion of cultural activity in Scotland in the Seventies and Eighties, feeding off the psychic frustrations of this new and enlarged intelligentsia. The Sixties cosmopolitanism of Demarco and the Traverse, part harbinger of these changes and part echo of the world youth revolt, has been overtaken by the creation of an indigenous performing theatre, an infant movie industry and an endless outpouring of local writing talent. In effect this has been a declaration of cultural independence.

MacDiarmid set out in the Twenties to counter-attack against the New Unionist Consensus of Scottish Labourism by launching a cultural guerilla war in the shape of the Scottish Renaissance. But he was wrong in trying to create cultural independence solely through the revival of Scots, which had no great resonance among either the popular masses or most of the intelligentsia, and he was further wrong in trying to justify this tactical failure with a certain cultural snobbishness. A self-aware Scotland demands a popular culture which reaches out to the mass of the population. When the real Scottish cultural renaissance came in the Seventies, it was not a contrived exercise in Scottishness but the very fact of creating a popular local cultural life on stage, at the typewriter or on celluloid meant inexorably that it would by its own existence breathe independent life into the manufacturing of ideas about Scotland, about being Scots, and about the predicament of a thinking Scotland without a state to turn its aspirations into reality. Where MacDiarmid failed gallantly, the Mayfest, Women Live and 'Gregory's Girl' have succeeded: almost to a person the Scots cultural intelligentsia support Home Rule and the Scottish Workers' Republic in place of London state socialism.

This defection from Unionist Labourism has been reinforced by the growth of anti-Stalinist marxism and by the spread of feminism north of the border. These winds have affected not only Scottish Labourism but also its Communist Party ally, removing another prop from the rotting Labourist edifice. Till the Seventies, roughly a quarter of the entire membership of the British Communist Party was concentrated in the greater Glasgow area. While the CP was almost non-existent in that other bastion of Labourism, the English North East, in Scotland the CP was powerful in the unions, shop stewards committees and, latterly, in the STUC. The result was not a French or Italian-style running fight with social democracy. Rather, there was an alliance.

British Labourism is founded on the principle of the division between politics (i.e. elections) and trade unionism. The Labour Party fights elections, while the unions deal with wages and working conditions. This split results from the actual creation of the Labour Party by the unions as their 'watchdog' in Parliament. Elsewhere in Europe this division of labour does not occur. The European socialist parties established their respective union machines as adjuncts of their political machines to organise support, raise cash and make political propoganda effective through strikes. The British model leaves Labourism at a disadvantage. The Labour Party machine as such hardly exists outside of election times, for it has no other rationale for existence. Therefore there is no real transmission belt to mobilise working-class support for Labour policies. In Scotland, however, things were different because the mass CP used its weight in the factories to mobilise politically, and did so in the service of Labourism.

The Labour Party in Scotland got people elected to parliment and local government, and in return for tacit electoral support let the CP run the unions. There was a whiff of Cold War politics at the start of the fifties but mostly Scots Labourism was prepared to tolerate the CP. In fact there was a degree of 'mixing' of respective ideologies: Scottish Labourism is perhaps the most Stalinist variety of Labourism within the British state both in terms of political programme (long indistinguishable from that of the CP) and in terms of internal party regime.

This Labourist-CP amalgam has now shattered. Communist Party membership has collapsed as the post-Sixties generation turned to Trotskyism, feminist and other anti-bureaucratic creeds. The working class has been repelled by the police states of Eastern Europe associated with the Communist Party. The bastions of CP organisation in the shipyards, mines and engineering factories have been destroyed by de-industrialisation. The Scottish CP's political weight now depends only on its residual control of the apparatus of full-time trades union officials — bureaucrats cut off from the factory floor. These developments have left the Labourist machine in Glasgow an ageing head without a body.

This decay of the Labourist machine has been accelerated by a major revolution in the structure and demography of Labour's traditional voting base, the West of Scotland industrial working class. This was the proletarian heartland which the SNP tried and only just failed to storm in the mid-Seventies. What the SNP failed to do, Thatcher's recession is accomplishing. The core section of the working class, the base on which Scottish Labourism rested, lies in manufacturing and mining. Here were the strong unions, the CP-controlled shop stewards movement and the male, craft ethos. It is precisely this core section which has been cut to ribbons by the present slump. In 1974, one Scots worker in three was employed in mining and manufacturing. By 1982 it was one in four. In the last decade over two hundred thousand jobs have been wiped out in this area, never to return.

It must not be deduced from the above that the collapse of the set of alliances which have buttressed Labourist ideology in Scotland will sweep away the Labour Party as such. Instead, the erosion of the material basis and rationale for Labourism has precipitated a debate about the future role of socialism within the party, and about the new set of popular alliances it will be necessary to construct in order to defeat Thatcherism. One proposal, associated with CP intellectual and English historian Eric Hobsbawm, calls for a People's Alliance. That is for a popular bloc to rally support from any and all sections of the community opposed to Thatcher. Hobsbawm rightly devines the failure of orthodox Labourism, but his alternative People's Alliance is nothing more than an accommodation with the English professional classes achieved by abandoning those bits of Labourist programme the middle classes don't like — nationalisation, free collective bargaining and leaving the EEC. Shorn of the jargon, the People's Alliance means a coalition with the SDP on the latter's terms. Supporters of the People's Alliance would argue that since the only way to vote out Thatcher is by such a coalition, and since it is imperative to get rid of Thatcher, then it is necessary for socialists to forego their long-term objectives in favour of what can be achieved now.

But is not the real choice. The English petty bourgeois psychosis known as Thatcherism is merely the reflection of a real material crisis on the economic and social plane. A genuine alliance with the middle classes, which is not to be eschewed in principle, can only work if it is on basis of a programme which deals with the root causes of this crisis. Otherwise the trajectory of the Hobsbawm approach can only be to create a People's Alliance on the vague basis of 'common sense', English, middle class values, i.e. 'decency', the Dunkirk Spirit, Fabian paternalism, with the unemployed of the Eighties serving as a generation of new model evacuees from Thatcher's Blitz being fostered by the English gentry in an idyll of thatched cottages and country hedgerows. To invoke English 'decency' and the commonweal of This Island Race against Thatcher's nasty, lower middle class, grocer's shop concern for 'trade' is to tread a path away from socialism towards English populism. This is indeed Hobsbawm's project: to invoke English nationalism against Thatcher's sectional assaults on the working class and middle class. However, English nationalism is at root the tradition of Empire, of racism, of jingoism and of acceptance of caste. English populism is rotten to the core, and it is a strange direction to take for a Hobsbawm who once savagely attacked Tom Nairn for the supposed crime of capitulating to nationalism. Thus Hobsbawm's criticism exposed as English parochialism.

Yet here lies the clue to the future of Scottish politics. A new popular bloc must be created to replace traditional Labourism and oppose Thatcherism. But a Scots Home Rule Alliance rather than a so called People's Alliance. A united front that will mobilise all shades of working class and popular support around the democratic demand for the right of the Scottish people to decide their own affairs, and against the imposition of the will of a Tory government which has no mandate north of the border. The Home Rule demand is a body blow to the super-centralist English state and its constitutional convention of Parliamentary sovereignty rather than popular sovereignty. It changes the emphasis of leftwing politics from the strategy of the begging bowl of regional economic aid to the need to confront de-industrialisation through local initiative. That raises in turn the question of popular sovereignty over local Capital and the Multinationals. It transforms the role of the STUC and Scots trades union movement from that of supplicant in London to defender of working class interests at home. It will transform the secret monastic orders in St. Andrews House and the Scottish Arts Council into politically accountable servants of the Scottish working people. And above all the fight for Home Rule is based not on a reactionary imperial heritage but on a popular tradition of resistance to oppression and exploitation, the honourable 'national' tradition of the 1820 Rising, of Maclean, of Maxton.

Who will join this Home Rule Alliance? The very way in which Scottish Labourism's old alliances have disintegrated indicates how the alliance must coalesce. Already the Scots intelligentsia has opted for Home Rule. With the collapse of Labourist-Stalinist machine, the Labour Party faces the necessity of reorganising itself as a European-style compaigning party in order to mobilise a new constituency for itself. It can no longer be just an electoral machine. South of the border, this has given rise to the GLC phenomena: a local Labour Party turning to campaign politics and using the local government machine not as an end to itself but as a platform. The first signs of this development appearing in Scotland have been in the Lothians in the fight for the Labour Regional Council against Governor General Younger's dictats. Forced at long last to convince and persuade people rather than treat them as voting fodder, the Scottish Labour Party has become fertile ground for debating ideas which would once have been dismissed as heresy. Witness the emergence of George Galloway, not as a Labour Town Council boss — though he is — but as a veritable ideologue actually debating political strategy at the level of theory. Can you imagine a Labour Glasgow Lord Provost doing that in the Fifties and Sixties? This cultural revolution has attracted a steady flow of recruits from the left of the SNP and it is now perfectly possible to find Labour Party members who are not simply pro-devolution but pro-socialist independence.

What of the mass of the working class as part of a Home Rule Alliance? Scotland never had the Midlands, mass production industries with their conservative, and Conservative-voting, highly skilled, highly paid workers. The latter have become demoralised by incomes policies and unemployment and trooped into voting lobbies for Thatcher. The Scots workers reacted to the onset of crisis by supporting the SNP, i.e. by calling for radical democratic solutions. The rightwing, Poujadist leadership of the SNP could not respond to this gut reaction, and so the workers have temporarily returned to Labourism (spurning the SDP en route). This experience of the early Seventies shows that there is the makings of a Home Rule Alliance based on the workers movement.

Some have taken the decline in the core section of the industrial working class as signalling the end of political projects based on this stratum. This is a profound error. Every capitalist slump recasts the shape of the working class, but it does not eliminate the worker. For instance, it was the post-war expansion of the proletariat that brought massive numbers of women out of the home into work, preparing the ground for the rise of the Women's Movement. The smaller number of industrial workers today is merely the changing division of labour within the overall capitalist order, and those who continue to live by selling their labour power will still have nothing to lose but their redundancy payments. From Lee Jeans to Timex, Scots workers continue to show a traditional syndicalist reflex for direct action which is absent south of the border. There is every likelihood that a recast workers movement will throw up a new leadership as part of the Home Rule Alliance, though this leadership might be very different from the archetypal male, manual, engineering shop steward.

Male engineering workers were not always the leadership of the workers movement: in the early nineteenth century it was the educated artisans; in France the lack of industrial concentration passed the leadership to socialist town councils rather than shop stewards. In the new microchip age the workers movement will adjust to changing times. Thus some would identify a new workers' leadership emerging among the computor workers, the skilled priesthood which capitalism cannot live without as once it could not live without the boilermaker. (And note that Scotland has gained a major share of the British electronics industry.) However the essence of working class leadership is the ability to mobilise other workers through the very mechanics of the production process which throws workers together. It was the ability of the engineers to lead the tens of thousands of workers under the same factory roof that turned them into the shock troops of the Red Clyde. Today small factory units render this model an unlikely variant, and the computor workers' monopoly of scarce skills will probably produce only a very well-paid conservative labour aristocracy. The reduction of the workforce into small units in fact explains the re-emergence of municipal socialism. Only the democratic, socialist commune can now act as a centraliser of working-class activity and resistance. This reinforces the need to build an alliance around the fight for an Assembly linked to socialist municipal authorities, and further requires the undermining of the traditional Labourist model of the use of local authority machinery as a base for power-broking with London.

How shall the Home Rule Alliance be formed? Since a Thatcher government will never freely grant the Assembly for which a majority voted in 1979, it will be necessary to emulate the tactics of the Irish Home Rule movement. The sovereign will of the Scottish people is already expressed in their democratically elected representatives. These representatives, or as many as respect the mandate of the 1979 referendum, must convoke a convention to demand the Assembly and challenge the right of the Thatcher government to dictate to the Scottish working people. Such a convention should embrace MPs, Regional, Island and District Councillors. Most would be from the Labour Party, but other political parties could be shamed into attending. A mass public campaign would be necessary to get such a convention. Primarily it would be necessary to mobilise and win over the Labour Party and the STUC.

The present Campaign for a Scottish Assembly is unlikely to prove the catalyst for such a movement. The CSA is cast too much in the mould of the apolitical Covenant movement of the Fifties: too middle class, too Protestant, too male, too middle-aged. In other words hardly representative of the real Scotland of the working people or the radical intelligentsia. Perhaps the initiative might come from the concerted action of such bodies as the Scottish Labour Co-ordinating Committee, the Scottish Socialist Society, the John MacLean Society, and individuals on the Home Rule, anti-Thatcher left such as George Galloway and Stephen Maxwell. To argue the case there is the beginning of a serious radical Home Rule press in the shape of *Radical Scotland, Cencrastus* and *the Bulletin of Scottish Politics,* though there remains the lack of a working-class weekly of the stature of the old *Forward.*

Such a campaign would only succeed over the dead body of Scottish Labourism. But for those of us within the Labour Party today the death of Labourism is the birth of a new mass socialist Labour Party based on campaign politics. With great respect to those inside the SNP, the choice is neither a socialist party without Home Rule nor a Home Rule party before socialism, but a party of both. The SNP cannot be a multi-class, 'national' party and embrace socialism. Neither socialism nor Home Rule are achievable without the Scottish working class. The collapse of the SNP vote and the attempted expulsion of the '79 Group point only to the conclusion that it is necessary to build a Home Rule current within the Labour Party. The ideological crisis of Labourism means there has never been a better time to do this. The condition of success will be to convert the constitutional relationship of the Scottish Labour Party to the British Labour Party to one of federalism, in which an autonomous Scottish (Independent?) Labour Party forms an equal coalition with a separate English sister party.

Can it really be done? Some years ago, I sat in the proverbial smoke-filled room and argued with the now Chairperson of the Scottish Labour Party, Gordon Brown, over the slate for a student election. Disagreement prevailed over whether to nominate a soggy left candidate or a Trot (me). I remarked we were on the horns of a dilemma. No, no, said Gordon, for a marxist there should be no such thing as a dilemma, merely a choice. Quite right, Gordon. Scotland has never been socialist. But the choice is there.

George Kerevan

DAVID BLACK

'THE PREDICAMENT OF THE SCOTTISH WRITER'
— Some Random Reflections

The first predicament of the Scottish writer, invited to write about his or her condition, is to decide how to sex his or her pronouns. Pending the discovery of an acceptable generic pronoun, I suggest that the male writers should use *he* as the generic form, females *she* — not at all a satisfactory solution, but I can see no better one. If, therefore, I use *he* rather than *he or she,* throughout these reflections, I hope it will be recognised as an attempt to avoid a tedious stutter, and not construed as a subtle insult to women.

'The Scottish writer' confronts a confusing scene. Jean-Paul Satre once said: 'No man is a waiter'; by the same token nor is anyone a Scottish writer. We are all individual human beings first, and writing and Scottishness are secondary characteristics, capable of wide variation. Ian Fleming was a Scottish writer, in some sense; it's hard to believe he belongs in the same species as Hugh MacDiarmid. So I shall narrow the focus of the phrase, and assume it refers only to writers of what aspires to be 'literature'.

Such writers have a very special importance. More than anyone else, they are the people who bring consciousness to the experience of their community, celebrating its distinctive characteristics in a way that allows for an appropriate pride, and often discovering far in advance of others the neglected areas or the growing points. The development of a country's literature is a crucial element in the development of a differentiated national self-awareness.

In that last sentence I deliberately play with the words *country* and *nation*. For the paradox of Scotland is that she is a country but her people are not quite a nation. The writer who embodies the conflict of his community shares the uncertainty: he speaks for the rocks and cities of Scotland, but with whose voice does he speak and to whom? Sometimes he wonders if the 'Scotland' which obsesses him is a mere fantasy, and the reality is North Britain, only topographically distinct in the seamless garment of international Western consumerdom. Sometimes he wonders if his fantasy alone keeps Scotland in some tenuous being. MacDiarmid put it memorably:

Is Scotland nothing then
But the will of certain men?

Will his preoccupation with Scotland prove fertile in the long run, or is it all a hiding to nothing, in which case he has misread the tea-leaves and would do better to jack it in and become a chartered accountant, like all other sensible Scots?

And what is the relation of all this to his personal life? After all, like everyone else, he has only a few decades into which to crowd friendship, fun, the opposite sex, family life, money, power, etc., and the devouring claims of 'achievement' become, by a paradox, limitless when the achievement itself can take no very certain shape. It may be too that as a writer his gifts don't lie in the political direction. Yeats said that Ireland needed her independence in order to free her poets from obsession. The energy poured by her writers into Scotland is also a sort of pathological drain, and yet only by this willingness to suffer is Scotland's identity maintained.

'A Scottish poet maun assume/The burden o' his people's doom'. That makes it sound like a choice!

From another angle: Scotland has three languages. Scots and Gaelic at once restrict you: write in one of them and you know your readership is local. The limitation is narrowness; the gain is definition. Write in English and heady visions of all Anglo-America open up before you. Yeats and Joyce did it for Ireland; why should Anglo-America not be interested in Scotland?

No question it isn't, however. Perhaps we had our day, at the time of Burns, Scott, Bryon, and in the world's eyes are forever fixed in it. Now Bill Forsyth's *Local Hero* (alas, straight out of the kailyaird) is the nearest we get to attention. This is not a conspiracy; it is the case.

Why is Gaelic so neglected? Mention it (mention Sorley MacLean) outside Scotland, and you are met with the polite silence which is a signal that we-are-of-course-indulgent-to-your-hobbyhorse-and-will-be-happy-to-resume-the-conversation-when-you-get-off-it. Gaelic is older than the Nordic and Romance level of the modern European languages and perhaps one is meeting here some deep bone-level of tribal antipathy. To the English-speaker, Gaelic is more foreign than French or German, and even than Greek or Russian, which at least have a place in his map and sense of history. Gaelic *does not exist.* (Culturally, in Europe, the Roman Empire has never been superceded.)

Still more puzzling is the neglect of Scots. This is perfectly easy for an English-speaker to read; and MacDiarmid's lyrics, most of Garioch's poems, etc., are of unmistakable excellence. Anglo-America knows of Heine and Rilke, but not of *Sangschaw* and *Penny Wheep!* Perhaps, where Gaelic is too foreign, Scots is not foreign enough: it encounters the resistence we feel to taking seriously poems in Cockney or Zummerzet.

However, writers in Scots and Gaelic know very well they are aiming for a local readership. Writers in English are less clear about this. We have to locate ourselves in the huge territory of the English and American (etc.) literatures. There is an interesting detail here to do with social class. In England, literature is associated with the upper-middle classes. A writer, regardless of his actual background, gravitates toward that position in society, and seems to speak with that sort of voice and authority. In Scotland, the gravitational pull is towards the 'working-class' (though that is too modern a phrase to catch the nuance I really want). The robust mockery of Burns and MacDiarmid against social pretension is always echoing somewhere in the writer's mind. I suspect many Scottish poets share my immediate gut aversion to the likes of Auden and Betjeman, which is really based on this sort of class-prejudice. I had very consciously to *learn* to admire Auden (whom now I regard as a great poet). All this despite the fact that I myself come from the anglicised middle classes. — It is often easier to relate to Americans, with whose prejudices we have less connexion.

Scottishness remains a stumbling block. *Scots are very different.* We are more serious, we are more inclined to speak plainly, there is in most of us a bitterness that will not enjoy the bland assurance of those who feel themselves to be masters in their own home. We have the mentality of the colonised, and it is as apparent in our denials of bitterness *(Local Hero* again!) as it is in the ranting and intentionally bitter passages in MacDiarmid. The English, understandably, have no desire to hear that note; Americans are intrigued and rather surprised — 'Gee, I thought Whitehall was run by Scots'.

So to write in English is paradoxical. It gives access to the world beyond the Scottish border; but it also disguises the real differences. I come back yet again to the political falsehood of the 'United Kingdom' — a collective denial of difference which cannot be rectified by the action of individuals only.

How far is all this generalising on insufficient evidence? How far am I speaking for people with some personal gripe, which they rationalise as 'Scotland's wrong'? How far am I affected by my private sense of not-belonging, as a man who had left behind three countries before ever I came to Scotland at the age of 8?

For perhaps the crucial predicament of the Scottish writer is to get Scottishness into proportion. There will always be things that are unsatisfactory in the way a society is run — if I were English I should live in a chronic state of rage against the class-system, which makes it abominably difficult to meet people on the level, person to person. No doubt these things deserve to be raged at, but meanwhile one has a life to live, and 'to be choked with hate/May well be of all evil chances chief' — bitterness may be worse than the affliction that calls it forth.

It sounds unheroic, but it is also important to be able to get on with other things, to know where one stands on the principal Scottish issues but also to recognise that unless the Scottish people are prepared to do something about them, then nothing will happen. The lamentable outcome of the devolution referendum points to the sheer dullness of imagination which prevades Scotland (and whatever one may think of the '40% rule' it wasn't wholly unreasonable — most organisations require more than a simple majority to change the constitution). If, even when offered the opportunity on a plate, the actual population of Scotland votes against it, or fails to grasp it firmly, then the writer has to avoid fixation and look somewhat elsewhere. 'Great indeed,' says the *I Ching,* 'is the meaning of the time of retreat.' (And the commentator adds: 'Retreat is not to be confused with flight'.)

I have written most of these notes at a rather high level of subjective generality. More tangible, for the writer, is the problem of finding a market, or an audience. London publishers, editors, and readers are not interested in the same concerns as Scots — to what extent does the Scottish writer wish to adapt himself to appeal to them?

One of the reasons which makes me optimistic that a change *is* about to develop in Scotland, is that the situation on this front is changing. Coming events cast their shadows before, and one such premonitory shadow is, in my opinion, the development over the past two decades of sounder Scottish publishers and journals. Scotland *is* acquiring a voice, almost in spite of herself. Twenty years ago, nationalism looked, and often behaved, like a strident and eccentric belief, and most of the writers concerned for it had a worrying tendency to be alcoholic. Nowadays, it has come in from the cold, and, at any rate in the moderate form of 'devotion', it is respectable in any company. — Meanwhile the English, having 'lost their illusions' and their idealism, have become a far less admirable people. Here is one predicament which is waning.

And here is one which is on the increase. If greater autonomy for Scotland is now something of a likelihood, will it prove a benefit or a misfortune? Will the theoretical and dogmatic tendency of the Scots, which formerly made them vulnerable to the miserable rigours of Calvinism, now make them vulnerable to the equally high-minded and no less miserable rigours of a dogmatic Socialism? (There are certain parallels, conceivably, between the lack of personal freedom, economic incompetence, lofty rhetoric, and general depression of the modern Soviet Union, and the rather similar elements in pre-Union Scotland.) Will the enormous emigration of talent from Scotland over the past three centuries mean that dullness prevails, whether or not Scotland is 'free'? — If I were dictator of the new Scottish republic, I should be strongly tempted to import a few hundred Soviet Jews, to increase the talent of the country, and to unite its imagination with world history!

But such issues will then not be predicaments. Where one is free to make decisions, and to act, then for better or worse life can go forward. The true predicament is when individual freedom is blocked by a 'bad' collective situation, and the individual is then unable to play the role in society to which his talents and disposition call him. This is certainly to some extent the case for the Scottish writer. It would be wrong, however, to conclude without pointing out that one's predicaments are also one's opportunity. All things are grist, to the man with a sufficient mill. No greater Scot will arise than Hugh MacDiarmid, and he lived his whole life in the United Kingdom.

David Black

TESSA RANSFORD

WORKERS IN THE SPIRIT

At a conference on the economics of poetry in the countries of the EEC, the representative from Greece explained that in his country poets are considered workers like everybody else, making an essential contribution to political life (ie the life of men and women as socially and communally organised) but that they are thought of as 'workers in the spirit'.

I suspect that most people who think in English have a rather emaciated view of the word 'spirit', and that therefore to call a poet a 'worker in the spirit' would, in their mentality, *dis*associate him or her from social or political involvement. This is a result of the dualism engendered in our culture by a misunderstanding of Plato and a platonisation of Christianity. The Descartian maxim that thinking makes us human also contributes to this, especially when thinking itself is understood as something we do when *not* active or emotional. We are beginning to know better now, in the age of computers, realising that consciousness is more comprehensive and complicated than the process of thinking as such, and that *psyche* and *soma* are vitally inseparable.

At St. Paul's disposal were six words to describe the various components or aspects of human existence: *psyche* and *soma*, (soul and the form it takes) *nous* and *kardia* (intellect and heart/feelings) *pneuma* and *sarx* (spirit and flesh). We tend to reduce these to two, and place them in opposition, whichever of the six we may be using. Thus *psyche*, *nous* and *pneuma* get lumped into one as 'spirit' and *soma*, *kardia* and *sarx* get thrown together as 'matter' or 'flesh'. The word *pneuma* means also breath or wind and is the life-giving power or energising force of the whole. It is closer in meaning to our more old-fashioned use of it as in 'a spirited horse' or being in 'high spirits'. This is the way Plato used it too. Spirit is a full-blooded and full-brained concept, not an airy invisible 'cloud' that escapes the 'prison of the flesh' and is superior to the efforts of the intellect. The Jews were commanded to love God with all their *mind* and *strength* as well as heart and soul, and none was considered less important than any other. To worship God 'in spirit and in truth' must have meant with action, effort and intelligence, freely and independently of particular places, people and rituals; and love of God was inseparable from involvement with one's fellow human beings on the face of the earth.

It seems fairly clear that most poets in Scotland do not think of themselves as 'workers in the spirit' nor are they considered such by the community. This is partly because people associate 'spirit' with 'religion' and religion with 'the church'. It is too important a word not to be rescued from these confines. Spirit, if it is worth the name, permeates every blade of grass and cobble-stone of the body politic, giving each thing its 'thisness', and the whole its vitality. It is not going to let itself be trapped and pinned down into any mechanical or organisational institution, nor can it be manipulated into social 'good causes'. It is unpredictable and irresistible. Workers in it can only make themselves available and be ready to act when the time comes. But they can also prepare the way by removing obstacles, dead wood and barriers of all kinds and making channels of free communication. (I have used 'it' when referring to the spirit, not to de-personalise its nature, but for lack of a suitable pronoun for that which is neither male nor female, Jew nor Greek, but can work through all things and people in a manner appropriate to the time and place, becoming visible only in its effects).

Poetry is of the highest possible importance to society. This is not to set it on a pedestal, or confine it to universities or elitist cliques. David Jones, poet and artist, has renamed homo sapiens as 'Man the Signwriter', whose task is to live in such a way that he makes his own significance. We do not make this out of nothing, but out of the material to hand. Words are common, cheap, available. If anything, nowadays, they are an overwhelming threat, coming at us in undigested waves of nonsense through the media. In other countries and societies than ours, words have been precious, sacred and effective. In Russia, they are still respected and feared. Solzhenitsyn spoke, in his Nobel prize lecture in 1972, of 'one word of truth' saying that such a word could outweigh a world of lies. He has based his life on that belief. Mandelstam's poems were memorised by his friends. Great crowds listen to poetry readings and words are carried away in their minds and lives.

Scotland's poets have had spirit and still have spirit. Perhaps it is just because they realise their task is so daunting that they also tend to lack confidence in their ability, often transferring that into a lack of faith in the importance of their task. It is not easy to live at the disposal of the spirit. People in a pragmatic society cannot understand. They disapprove, object or laugh with embarrassment. I was once told, on applying for the use of premises for the School of Poets I founded in February 1981, that either we would be genuine poets and therefore disreputable, or we would be responsible people and consequently not genuine poets. I declined to reply.

This sort of attitude can provoke a brash showing-off, which is rightly not applauded in Scotland, or a retreat into proud isolation or humble insignificance. Both reactions are based on fear. Why are so few Scottish poets known outside Scotland? Why have our universities imported Peter Porter and Douglas Dunn as writers-in-residence? Which English univeristies have had Scottish writers-in-residence? Why are poets with the highest status in Scotland those who are published in England?

To be at the disposal of the spirit is no passive inactivity. It means extreme attention, intense receptivity and strenuous grappling with the meaning of events. It is this situation that the processes of the *Weltgeist* or collective unconscious or super-consciousness (Teilhard de Chardin's noosphere) can interact and infiltrate the individual consciousness. The works waiting to be written demand the life to be lived. We can't fit them in round other things.

Literature in Scotland has limitations because of its subservience to the dominant culture of England, in the face of which it feels less important, overlooked and misunderstood in language-experience and perception. Scottish writers are often geographically isolated, but many are also psychologically isolated, not knowing if they qualify as writers or not. A real lack of confidence, as opposed to a proper humility, can cause panic or paralysis. The result is that often mediocre and middle-of-the-road people are allowed to prevail, ignored by the talented perhaps, but with a following of the less talented who hope to get into the swim. The general public get tired of it all and switch off to modern literature altogether.

Scottish writers tend also not to feel they are contributing to a rich mosaic of culture, which Scotland does have with its three living languages and its mixture of races and diversity of landscape. Scotland can also independently relate both to the English-speaking world and to Europe. It looks too much still to London. Lack of confidence also forces writers to define themselves (or let themselves be defined) by categories and labels, especially when writing for the media. This is what Aristotle describes as being on the leading-rein! Women particularly suffer from this, and no less in the era of the new feminism. Feminism is a support-system encouraging women to be and become what they are or could be, as individuals and full human beings — in so doing giving men the same chance to avoid being stereotyed. However the compartmentalising mind of the masses (and the media) makes of feminism yet another stereotype, and women find they are expected to conform to a new set of rules. They must write as women rather than as poets. (I once had a poem returned by a male editor with the comment 'This is not a true women's voice!'

Writers in Scotland vis-a-vis England are in a situation analogous to that of women vis-a-vis men as writers since women also are often made to feel inferior and their peculiar insight misunderstood. How is a woman to know, for instance, whether she fails in an application for a job because she is really an inferior writer to the men who hold such posts, or because she is not regarded as a serious writer, or because she doesn't need the money if she has a husband or because she might actually be good enough to pose a serious threat to the ruling men of letters? Women with foreign names or a flippant, entertaining style are more acceptable. But matters are not helped for serious women writers by interviews such as that in the *Scotsman* colour supplement (April 1983) with a successful woman writer who is reported as saying 'The time I get for writing is what's left over from everybody else' and that her writing is 'secondary to running a home and family'. (We are told that cleaners are employed, her sons are grown-up and her husband is a wealthy director of an oil company!) It is this kind of comment that makes the situation more difficult for women who put their writing first at whatever cost, who want or need to be self-supporting even if married, who clean their own homes and allow their husbands and sons not be dependent on them.

Of course, women have chores to be done and relationships that demand time and attention. Men have these also. The writer, being self-employed, often has to appear 'selfish' in order to keep working hours in a way that someone going out to work does not. Poetry is not a matter of churning out 6000 words a day on a word-processor, nor is there necessarily impressive amounts of research to be done (although there may be research and travel involved). Poetry is a way of life that demands following up ideas, often fruitlessly trying them out, working them through, revising, beginning again, with no regularity of routine or commissions in advance from publishers or the media. Highly inventive mathematicians and creative scientists also work like this. They are thinking out formulae in the supermarket. It is not a condition exclusive to poets. But in comparison with producing robots or new weapons perhaps, poetry is not valued at all.

Ours is a pragmatic society — an aftermath of the Romans. We call something good if it can be proved useful, a means to some other end. We have therefore a developed technology — which is by definition a means to other ends. Money is a means to any end, as are computers. However, by this rating, the end we choose is only of value if it in turn leads to some other end. Ultimately, we have to admit that *something* is an end-in-itself, with intrinsic value. People obviously do unconsciously have this estimation of poetry as an end-in-itself because they expect poets to write it 'for its own sake' and not to be so obscene as to want paid or published! This is more emphasised with poetry than the other arts, which blatantly need money to be produced or performed. A pragmatic society, whose only standard of value is money, values least what is least expensive (that means-to other-ends test!) The vicious circle continues: any money spent on poetry, for the Poet's livelihood, the publishing, advertising and distribution of books, its presenting on radio or television, for providing facilities for consumers, setting up sevices and centres for learning and developing skills in it — these are all laughed to scorn! Genuine poets and their poetry shouldn't need such help! Again, no research has been done into the economic factors of poetry. Generalisations are bandied about as truths for all time: it is an elitist activity, a minority interest, and even that is too mysterious and sacred to interfere with! The EEC is sponsoring some research into Poetry and I hope that the Scottish Poetry Library Association will be able to undertake it and make the findings available. I do know that some research into what elderly people in Dumbiedykes wanted by way of adult education showed that, after local history and swimming, poetry came third in their list!

One way in which I have tried to ease the deadlock is to begin the process of establishing a poetry library for Scotland. This is envisaged as a centre of information, a meeting point, the focus for people interested in and involved in poetry, a means of generating events and tours and visits, and a place where small press publications may be found. The potential public for poetry is untapped, partly because those who are slightly interested but feel they are too ignorant, or who don't know whether they are interested or not, have no easy means of finding out!

The tendency to feel inadequate about poetry is not confined to those without degrees in English literature! Teachers, lecturers, editors and producers often feel uneasy about poetry. They may have had no initiation at all into Scottish poetry through their education so that there is a desperate need to make this more available. There is no rule of thumb by which to judge new poetry and so it is a risk for producers, editors and teachers. They will play safe and use anthologies or poets published by the big four: Oxford, Penguin, Faber and Secker (although I've yet to read a good poet published by the last!) Some rule of thumb might be found in the formula: *the form should be married to the content and the content should be of universal significance for life.* It is certainly better that too much poetry be available than too little. The dregs will quickly sink. This playing-safe attitude has helped to perpetuate the mediocre male voice in much of recent British poetry which in comparison with almost any other English-speaking country, not to mention the poetry of other languages, appears less vital, experimental, interesting and significant for the life of humanity on earth.

The Nobel-prize winning Greek poet, Elytis, is quoted as saying 'Poetry is a source of innocence full of revolutionary forces.' If we believe that society, when it is alive, is growing and changing, and that it can change for the better; and if we want to find an innocent way of achieving that life change, we should not despise poetry. But that is not its justification. It has such life-changing effects, like the other arts, precisely because it is an end-in-itself and of intrinsic value. But as Shelley says, it does need cultivation. It is not a natural weed. It needs the right milieu, a centre and an environment where it can flourish.

To sum up: Poetry deals in signs, like all art, using words as its material. Signs deal with human significance. In past years we have become dazzled by neon signs and have trivialised our talents and minimalised our value as human beings. A sense of our own significance is more important for human survival than oil or nuclear weapons. Our powers of destruction, stemming from fear, rage and guilt, have been made 'outward and visible' in the bomb and the economy that supports it. But we have discovered that every cosmic particle is balanced by its opposite. We must, therefore, have enormous powers of construction and creativity. We have laid cables, built many bridges, manufactured computers and machines of all kinds. We have laboured to prepare massive means to whatever ends we choose. But we know that all is coming to a halt and we are stopping to ask ourselves what are the ends we choose. What is human life and where does its value lie? We have to admit we are in the dark. Poetry can help to switch on the light. All the arts can do this, but poetry, using words, underlines and interprets them all. It is for poets to accept the challenge and broaden their minds to encompass the concept of liberty for themselves first and then for others. They must free themselves of labels and 'leading reins', and, in all humility and vulnerability, encourage each other to play a part in society as 'workers in the spirit'.

In his long poem *'Bread and Wine'* the German eighteenth century poet, Hölderlin, wrote 'und wozu Dichter in dürftiger Zeit?' which I have freely translated as 'What use are poems in a time of cut-backs?' I have written a poem on this theme, which is also the theme of this essay, in the ancient Greek alcaic metre which was a favourite of Hölderlin's:

In parsimonious times who will plead for poets
When bread and circuses must be paramount?
Expediency makes tall excuses
Debts do not die, nor residual hunger.

Our human life is dear and we pay the toll
By pining slowly, starved of Parnassian grass
That goats will crave and sheep discover
Sweeter than flowers in polluted meadow.

It is for their dear life, and not theirs alone
That poets write, whose unknown petitioners
Will draw abundant strength they need from
Generous gamblers with life worth living.

Not use, perhaps, but wont, gives the poet room,
But cannot place him save as a therapist.
Repairs are not his task, but making
Worlds out of words without recreation!.

Tessa Ransford

GEORGE GUNN

ATTACK: THE NEED FOR A SCOTTISH WRITERS CO-OPERATIVE

Let there be no misunderstanding about this: literature is under attack. The creative force is clashing with the economic climate and as they collide, Art suffers. Poetry has been thrown out into the shadowy boundaries and left to die. Such is our society's value judgement on this heightened art form. The state of poetry publishing in Scotland, 1983, is a sad reflection of the short sightedness and almost paranoid fear of this society's ruling elite that they treat poetry and almost all literature in this manner. They seem fearful of its very roots, unaware, it would seem, that their mismanagement of 'society' produces the most profound and political poetry and prose, not to mention theatre. In times of social and political repression, the *writing* flourishes. The *publications* does not.

As it stands at the moment, economic stringency dictates quite nicely what does and does not get published. This form of soft censorship is particularly insidious and unfortunately affects the Scottish writer more than most. The two phrases 'won't sell' and 'uncommercial' put the kiss of death on any book that a publisher sees as a bit risky. There is no such thing as taking a chance any more. The avenues of expression are being closed and subsequently the intellictual climate is in a temper of iron. This predicament brings up the basic question of freedom which Farquhar McLay so eloquently summarised in his essay *Art And Anarchism,* when he wrote:

> 'Artists and writers are there to ask questions: they are there to empathise with all kinds of people, to explore every kind of human situation, to fetch up into the light of day things which are collectivist ego, the nationalistic ego, the class ego and the occupational ego strive to keep hidden. It is out of these questionings and explorations that art gets made, that experience is accumulated. If man is not free to be an artist, if he is not free to make things on which he can put his signature, so to speak, then he is not free at all.'

So, the writer, being denied the right to publish what he/she wants when he/she wants to, is being denied an elemental freedom.

Unfortunately, for the writer, the future does not promise better circumstances. The eighties do not look like a pretty decade to be in. *All* culture is being thrown to the financial wolves and quite unmercifully devoured, as the bourgeois aesthetic of commercial profit reduces the asperations of the writer and artist to the merely pecuniary level of the capitalist system. Publishers in Scotland, for example, seem to have *survival* tatooed onto the foreheads of their subconscious. By adopting this myopic philosophy, publishing has quite simply failed the people it set out to serve — i.e. the writer and the public. It has failed the writer because new writing is getting harder and harder to publish and it has failed the public by not allowing them the opportunity to have at hand a comprehensive collection of contemporary writing.

This raises the question: what is present commercial publishing out to do, whom are they out to serve? It would appear, in the light of the arguments above, that they are only interested in serving the financial society that ensures their survival; they are putting the pound before the poem. It would also be safe to assume that if publishers in Scotland have a genuine desire to see Scottish literature flourishing as it should, then they should be publishing more of quality and innovation. That may seem a pretty obvious thing to state but a mere fact that it had to be stated is saddest thing of all. Publishers have no genuine desires, except in regard to money, then the desire is maximum.

How do you make poetry, and literature in general, popular? For example, how to take what John Berryman described as a 'language so twisted and posed in a form/that it not only expresses the matter in hand/but adds to the stock of available reality', (although Berryman attributed the above to one 'Jean Bennet') and make it accessible to what MacDiarmid would have called 'the commonality'? The answer must lie in new forms of publishing and distribution. Fresh ground has to be explored if new work is to reach a wider public than is currently allowed.

It would seem to me that the book trade is still too steeped in the traditional class structure and operated around the chauvinistic and coercive values of the past to have much to offer in the way of making literature truly popular. We have come to a situation where writers have to think hard and long about what it is they are responsible for and whom they are reponsible to. The monster of 'bourgeois individualism' has to be put to death. It is no longer enough just 'to make it'. We must commit what McLay describes as the 'ultimate subversion'. That is, writers must realise that current publishing methods invite/them both to fear and love the system, when in actual fact what the writer should be doing is transcending the system and according to Jean Paul Sartre; 'The revolutionary philosophy must be a philosophy 'of transcendence.'

The current sad situation Scotland finds itself in both politically and socio-culturally dictates that we have to break free from the traditional methods of book publication and distribution in order to secure a future for Scottish literature. It would be a tragedy if temporary needs somehow obscured the long-term plight of the Scottish writer. Selfish gain has to be guarded against if anything of value is to emerge. 'Writers languishing in an unpublished state should try and see beyond their own particular predicament to a more general appraisal of what has gone wrong: which is that not much is getting published; not a lot of books are being sold to the bookshops and bought by the public. Distribution networks and booksale outlets have all either collapsed or dried up to anything new, subsequently betraying art. Obsolete means are being employed to further dynamic ends and the ends are suffering untold damage. It would be easy to suppose that the problem is either economic or political, but that would be approaching the issue from only one level. As I see it, at the moment, the writer is denied the capability to do what Kropotkin envisaged when he wrote of the 'masses' to have 'realised their artistic and constructive genius which, at the present time, we see as the best guarantee of a still loftier evolution of our race'.

It is with mixed feelings that I announce that the technological revolution is with us. My own humble opinion is that the 'state' will see to it that this 'revolution' is made to perpetrate the status quo of intellect and ideas. What I embrace is the persuasion that if we, as writers, want to ensure the continuing existence of the printed word then we must embrace that revolution and see how it can further the aims of literature. The revolution has to be put to work. Writers, publishers, distribution agents and booksellers all have to wake up to the fact that we are emerging from the death throes and smouldering embers of one culture and entering into the age of fingertip availability and a new culture. The forces at work which create our literature had better realise this quickly if they want to bring literature back in from the periphery and closer to the mass of the population.

So, publishing must change and change radically. It is an awareness and embracing of new concepts that is needed. It is my view that if publishing is to continue to be of any significance at all then the writers must accept the responsibility for the production of books as an intrinsic facet of the entire socio-economic-organism which entails and manifests itself in the production of a 'book'. Quite emphatically: the producers have to take over the means of production. In 1838, the German anarchist Rudolf Rocker wrote, 'Only in the realm of economy are the workers able to display their full strength, for it is their activity as producers which holds together the whole social structure and guarantees the existence of society.' If you substitute the word 'worker' for 'artist' and the word 'social' for 'artistic' you will see what I mean.

But how to channel this need for change into something which will actually work for the writer and also allow he/she to *transcend the system*. It was to this end that a group of writers met in Edinburgh in January 1983 and decided to set up the Scottish Writers Co-operative. The primary objective of the Co-operative would be, it was decided, to fill the space which has been left by commercial publishing and to infuse a sense of honesty back into the methods of publishing and *distribution*.

So far the Scottish Writers Co-operative is a co-operative of intent only, having produced nothing in print. The important thing is that that intent is *real* and it will, given time, manifest itself in something important and vital. What is most important is the desire and right of the writer to be free to express (that *'elemental freedom'*) and what is vital is that writers break away from the sterotype of what is the common conception of publishing, that bourgeois aesthetic which invites the writer to 'both fear and love the system' which I mentioned earlier. Writers have to search and explore the possibillities of new forms for their work and this can only be achieved when the collective will is there. The Scottish Writer Co-operative offers the writer a chance to be in control and if this aim is achieved then we will truly have 'transcended the system'.

At this stage the Scottish Writers Co-operative, like the Scottish Socialist Society, is only a meeting place for ideas, but if the ideas and the message are transmitted and circulated then more writers will join and the Co-operative will get off the ground and begin to publish new and exciting work, to create that 'ultimate subversion'. What the Co-operative is bound to succeed in doing is to show up the established publishers as being ideologically bankrupt. They are restricted by their very existence, by their manic commitment to making money and their terror of anything new and, ultimately, they exist for themselves because they deny and ignore the needs of the people. What they produce is nice safe escapist fiction, trite elitist poetry that says nothing and woolly middle-class drama. This, of course, is the dictum of the State and it is to the State that every publisher has to look in case they step out of line. It's quite humourous the way the State invents methods of suppresion like 'pornographic' and even 'blasphemy'. (Blaspheme against what? Christian State censorship? Then I'm all for blasphemy). The straitjacket situation dictated by the State is a curb on the freedom of expression and it is a brutal and dead dogma. By maintaining it we end up with what Nietzche feared when he wrote: 'Culture and the State — let no one be deceived about this — are antagonists: the Culture State is merely a modern idea.'

What we have in 1983 is a State controlled and vetted culture and it is made to work by the 'economic stringency' which I referred to earlier. But this 'culture' is only the tip of the iceberg and it is merely what the majority of the people are allowed to read. What the Scottish Writers Co-operative must do is to make more people aware that there is a mass of new and exciting writing which they are being denied the right to read and which will never see the light of day if present publishers carry on in their own destructive way. Emily Dickinson wrote: 'Denial is the only fact received by the denied.' If the Scottish Writers Co-operative can make people realise that they are being *denied* the right to read new material then I feel things could change dramatically.

The basic idea behind the Co-operative is that the producers — i.e. the writers — must form an organisation which enables them to better their chances of realising their right to freedom of expression, which is publication. Also the Scottish Writers Co-operative must embrace and enforce certain demands upon itself which are, firstly and crucially: that its members, who are the producers, must safe guard and emphasise their right to that freedom of expression. Secondly (and the most practical) that the Co-operative must acquaint the writer with the technical management of production, which is publication, and the economic realities of the process in order to prepare them to take over the means of production; this would be Sartre's 'philosophy of transcendence' put into practice.

The Scottish Writers Co-operative must persuade writers to snap out the lethargy which is the attitude to the present restrictions. To 'snap' requires radical change and the only metre of change is to compare what went before to what has come to pass and my hope is that what the Scottish Writers Co-operative will manage will make the past appear unrecognisable. That, of course, is the nature of revolution.

Space does not permit me to go into the mechanics of how the Scottish Writers Co-operative proposes to function, i.e. the practicality of manuscript reading, money, etc. so it only leaves me to add that any information concerning the Co-operative can be obtained from Colin Mackay, 5 Warriston Terrace, Edinburgh, from George Gunn, 28 Cathcart Place, Edinburgh, or from the Editor of this magazine. I urge all writers who have read this article to join the Scottish Writers Co-operative. Only with the strength of unity can we enforce change and changes have to be, or we die.

George Gunn

DAVID BLACK

PARSIFAL PART ONE*

Age 45 I lay upon my sofa,
the bones I had conveyed to many places
gone slack within me, and reviewed my life.
I was the widow's child: it was in Melrose,
under the Eildon Hills, I had my birth.
It seems to me I could have other childhoods,
or have been conceived in other wombs than Maggie's!,
and sometimes (O, poor Scotland) I regret you,
your weather, bitterness, and narrow faces —
but that is how it was: the mountain Michael
Scott split threefold to confuse our passions
exerted on my youth its clover gravity —
and no doubt to my history of fickleness
added its mite. It could be from some ballad:
'the mountain threefold and the mother one',
an eerie juxtaposition. And my early
memories are of that shifty mountain:
one time some aunt or grandmother uplifted
my infant shoulders and — oops-daisy! — swung me
out of doors, at night, to view the staggering
cliffs of cloud about an absolute moon —
and to her left those speechless, breathing summits.
Or on July's high-arching summer days
I met the turf and tormentil of Scotland,
crawling about, blunt-legged, upon their skirts.

I mind, I mean remember, first the physical:
the washed bright tiles before the open backdoor
drying then to shreds of wetness: or the kitchen,
its grate black-leaded, and its fire-irons sparkling
brass at the handle changing to soot-black
at those unreachable ends that had no boundary;
and the rooms' lay-out possessed an awesome starkness,
to right the bathroom, and to left my mother's
high Calvinist bedroom, tall chairs, the tufted bedcover,
in bleak perspectives of knobbed polished floorboards.
Such were my early ikons. Were they for themselves, or as some metaphor describing
mother's body, no longer known with such
precise concreteness? I should not care to answer.
These were the givens and the world's on-goingness,
like her, the Eildon Hills, and Scotland's history,
to which I woke, and which I pass the buck for.

Yet mother's body does not wholly slip my
recollection. A lined and warted woman,
tall, not un-handsome, with a stately carriage
and golden voice — how often in my childhood
I was to inexpressible realms transported
hearing her sing as she went about the housework.
She told me stories too: of how beneath the
Eildon Hills King Arthur's men lie sleeping,

waiting the day when Scotland's future ruler
shall enter at the Lucken Hare and grasp
Excalibur; and then will wind the horn.
(And woe betide him who snarls-up the sequence!)
Or of the little people, called good neighbours,
though often naughty ones!, who tie their cream-white
tiny horses under the ringing bells
of the gorse in season, then all night
dance beside Ellen Water. These old stories
she loved and laughed with. Yet when I came in
enchanted to have met beside the burn
(age 4) the fairies skipping — she was contemptuous!;
and told me 'not to be so silly!', then,
when I persisted, 'not to tell such lies!'
Baffled I learned the skills of her duplicity.

I lived till age 15 under the aegis
of illness — 'imminent death' was my companion,
despite appearances. My father, dead in
battle, and two, much-elder, brothers, shot down
above the Netherlands, perhaps explained
my mother's hyper-caution. There was also
a base in fact for her sustained anxiety:
age 2 I had fallen ill and been unconscious
and in cold sweats and flushing fevers for
four days continuously — to her alarm
and terror lest her last remaining man
be taken from her. She decided therefore
that I was damaged, must not go to school
or mix with others, but must be protected
and nurtured only by her salving hands.
Under this strict or arguably permissive
regime I was brought up: by mother's house,
by countryside and Kirk I set my bearings,
and in rude health I flourished and abounded!

— As for the Kirk I shall not speak of it!
Intolerable abuse of God and time
and word, insult to all creation's many-
bodied and marvellous perfections, it was
a black affront to infancy's receptiveness.
I spit it like a stone out of these memoirs!

Yet as I meditate those early years
I find depths beyond depths. Ostensibly happy,
in windless days upon the grassy Eildons,
or fishing secretly from alder thickets
into the shining Tweed, or on my bicycle
over the little Border roads that follow
as best they can the irresponsible burns —
these I remember. Yet not quite remembered
(or were they so faint-shadowy even then
as not to quite occur?) were in-the-house
strange moods and atmospheres, strange endless longings
connected with the smell of floor-polish,
or glints of picture glass. Or waking in tears,

in boundless grief to think of mother's dying,
to think of the decay of body and flesh,
to glimpse the years to come like vast unmoving
sucking maggots, all feasting, one by one
dropping away sated. I think now such conceptions
may have been hers, not mine, and I perceived them
because she would not. But this uses words
somewhat outwith their meanings. — Or I remember
(for let me pull the stops out on obscurity!)
the quality of her absence: when she was not
there she could be present like a substance,
a vapour, plucking the marrow from my backbone
and leaving me sat staring at the distance
like a straw doll with huge glass-button eyes;
or like poor Pierrot deceived by Columbine.

So thus the circular years. Not long nor short
but at once infinite and non-existent
those years of childhood. But I learned to read,
and on thin chains of wiry letters hauled
a greater, stauncher world into my ken.
Kings, peoples, dynasties, and other climates,
battles, and cutting edges, and raw blood,
these fed a hunger which I had no name for
and could not speak of. I remember once,
on God-knows-what manoeuvre, through the valley
successive armoured cars and transports thundered,
halting bewilderingly in Melrose! There I
saw the soldiers head to foot in khaki,
spats, belts, and berets, and those English voices
naked and strong! To me they might have come from
beyond Andromeda! or from within, from
some deep inner dream. I gazed upon them
worshipping, dumbfounded. And when they left
I could not bear it, prayed to the roaring engines,
to every tailgate and passing mudguard, to every
soldier who waved to me, a passionate prayer
to come again, to be my world, embrace me.

— But I was speaking of books. We have too little
considered what it means, this spiritual passion
to stretch imagination round the planet
and through the vast vaulted chambers of prehistory:
Cambrian, Ordovician, Silurian,
Devonian, Carboniferous — what redemptive power
I found in those lumbering, enormous syllables,
what roots, and what foundations. When I saw the
'mats of blue-green algae' rocking lightly
on the primal waters I was surely prouder
than a Jew remembering Abraham. How peripheral
to that huge pedigree
I and my mother seemed; and from the trunk
I drew a strength not easily to be glimpsed
in the circumferential twigs. O *little* Scotland!
how you have lacked the wonders I invoke for
full-living, easy-bodied, confident men,

confident women. Yes, of course, a dream;
yet by that dream alone I guide my life,
and when I lose it, all is despair and blackness.
I owe it, somewhere, to the pre-Cambrian algae.

And other things I read. The cells or history,
countries and centuries crowded with frantic detail,
engrossed and then released me; that Norman King
who fathered in his wanderings more than seventy
casual bastards struck me with astonishment!
Here surely was a different value-system,
not anywhere spoken yet there in his actions
and in his reception by so many women,
and in, let's face it, in that stolid recording
by meek historians. They could entertain it!
They shared this world on which they passed no judgment
and knew it — did they know it? — knew at least
enough about it not to press their enquiries.
'Hence', they said laughing, 'came the origin
of the name Fitzroy.'
But I knew nothing and my heart grew great
with mystery. Half my world filled up
with wordless silence.

                    One day I spoke of this
to my tall mother, asking what it meant
that this important King had impregnated
so many 'serving maids and farmers' daughters'.
We were in the kitchen. She responded
with a sudden giggle, then seriously informed me
that there were men 'who took advantage of
their high position to do what they pleased'. I
said: 'And is it such things, then,
that please men, Mother?' Like a trap her teeth
snapped and she shouted at me: 'Go upstairs at once and
wash your mouth out! Horrid boy!' — at which
I made my ritual exit. On my return
she told me I had hurt her very badly
and must, on no account, ever again,
speak of these matters.

                    Therefore I refrained
from speaking of them. Yet I knew thenceforward
that I could not remain in that entanglement
to be strangulated with beliefs and silences.
I turned to science. Tranquil, lovely science,
like a deep drink of cold and steadying water
to one sweat-stained and bloody from the battle,
you taught me then that clarity existed,
clarity, true kindness, and intelligence —
taught, or reminded. What worlds of Lepidoptera
or classifications of crystalline rock
I printed on my memory to create
islands in chaos. But now I sensed the understanding structure, the formal harmonies
of atom, solar system, cosmos even

(though there the theories reached beyond my conceiving),
and nothing checked me. My voracity
now seems to me prodigious. It was the time
when Crick and Watson raced with Linus Pauling
to build an accurate model of the basic
molecule of inheritance; and I marvelled
over that complex grammar, over that language
in which the universe utters its creatures.
I sing a hymn to you, science. Sole discoverer
of this great system in its inter-connectedness,
bringer of light and order to the depths
of vastness and minuteness, time and space,
you are the supreme composer: tens of thousands
write their notes into your gigantic symphony
which is not arrogant, nor is it humble,
but is simply there, and forever to-be-revised
by the newcomer-who-will-abide-by-the-rules.
Salvific enterprise to which nothing is alien,
generous receiver, never-exhausted giver,
you release nature's children from her bondage
lovingly, without contempt or frenzy.
If I called you Apollo we would know your godhood;
but whether your name is masculine or feminine
I am uncertain.

              And now my fortunes altered:
for in the Melrose Public Library
I met a botanist! Great, bearded Johnson,
how little of you is captured in that dainty
half-comic title! You were my first scientist,
and in your ebullient and casual manner
you cannot have known what potent seeds you scattered,
talking of 'training and career structure',
of the need for colleagues, and your disrespect for them!
I shall always remember that late-autumn evening,
dark falling as we strode along the glistening
roadway, tall beech-trees in a row along the horizon
against a lurid, toneless, tempestuous sky.
You stopped from time to time to demonstrate
hard fern, or the ridges on pine-needles,
and laughed abundantly. And I was drunk
on the cold, the gale, and your exuberance.
I never saw you again and yet for many
years I think it was your image I travelled with,
more vivid to me than much that I encountered.

That night returning late for supper — un-
precedented event! — I told my mother
about this meeting. I talked eagerly and
it did not occur to me to make apology.
She was in high anxiety, could hardly speak
and huddled standing by the Aga cooker,
a pan in her hand. When I spoke of Johnson,
his beard and laughter and high-spirited vehemence,
she fainted clean away! From her great height
she sank like the Titanic to the floor,

dropping the pan. Awestruck, I picked it up;
I could not for a moment approach closer
that melted heap of clothes and body and limbs
and classic marble face she had become.
Then as I hesitated she revived.

— Revived so suddenly I was repelled!
for still in that disorder, from the heap,
she spoke un-humanly. 'Your brothers and father
died their violent deaths because of greed and
hatred. It was my fixed benign intention
to guard you from that fate, to bring you up
in virtue and gentleness. But now I see
the devil stirs in you, that that same passion
wakes like a sleeping monster deep beneath
the ocean of your tainted, bestial blood.
I cannot hold you longer. Go, changeling!
Go, you obscene, blood-lusting avatar
of all that is most hideous in your ancestry!
Never return!' Then from this strange somnambulistic
bodiless fury she resumed her swoon.

When she came round I had unfolded her
and was dabbing her forehead with a dampened dishcloth.
What tenderness of grief in both our faces!
Yet with me (and I wonder! was it with her also?)
it was conscious hypocrisy: I did not
for the smallest instant forget that bitter sentence
or the harsh passion within it. And as we coo'd
in a sweet conspiracy of concern and nonchalance
— how natural it seemed! and quite un-meaning —
I knew the clock had struck: that come tomorrow
I should leave my mother's house and not return.

David Black

*This is the opening section of a much longer poem, still in progress.

IAIN CRICHTON SMITH

MY LAND

My land I wished so violently to leave
and when I'd left return to it again
that I was sick with longing, for my love
had formed the perfect diamond in the rain.

I sat uneasily inside the plane
watching the sun set elsewhere, hollow crown.
Touch down, I whispered, O please God, touch down,
I famished for that episode of green.

And know there is no sorrow worse than this
once to have erred, the error to remain
forever changeless and forever done.
And that was why I rushed across the grass

to where you were. What present in my case
could ever pay you for the past we own?

TO GLASGOW

I look out as the rails
point toward Glasgow, crossing
and intercrossing. The brick
factories loom, the cubes
of high rise flats tower
over the Clyde. The dead
drift from the slums nosing
towards Loch Lomond. There was
Lynch in his long shorts, swaying
in the hot ring, punching
rivets in his tall queen,
the silken one, impudent
stick-legged genius at work. I gaze
at fat women in windows
taking the air. Blades
flash momently on the rails, grass
and weeds cover them. Bridges
join the spawn of small shops
advertising rubber goods,
and vast vaginas. I cry,
Glasgow, over the luxury
of your waste, the lives
brewed extravagantly up closes
with Fuck the Pope on them, almost your
accomplishments in literature.
The train runs through black
tunnels, then is
in the white daylight of Queen St.
Sloppily dressed in navy blue
the collector takes my chewed ticket.
I walk out into the light
which shines on hammers beating down
walls among stopped clocks.

THE OLD LADY

The old lady walks through the field with a basket of wild raspberries.
She says, 'I have been here for a long time.
I have seen the foundations of many houses,
and I have seen the children in their cradles, the dead in their hearses.'
A lark drawn out on a string of light sings above her.
Lover after lover lies in the pleats of the ground
over which in delirium the rabbits camper
and where in wet thickets the weasel eels.
'So many names I have known,' says the old lady
as she passes the well of green water
with its long disused chain.
They have disappeared into the grasses, the lads of pairts,
and the housewives who hung out their mended laundry,
the giants with white dust on their dungarees
who laboured in quarries in the sunlight.
Suns have sunk like great red cartwheels.
The old lady walks home with her basket of wild raspberries
and the children rout for trout in the river
bare-armed, bare-headed, with blades of grass on their toes.

Iain Crichton Smith

MARTIN MARRONI

OFFSHORE WIND

The wind blows strong
towards the sea. It combs
the grass; I tag along
to where a pictish fort's low
earthworks ridge the cliff-edge
like a furrowed brow.

Here lookouts would have searched
the grey horizon for sea-raiders;
but not on such a day. I lurch
to face the wind. Behind a fence
cows pasture round a ruffled loch
on which a coracle would merely dance.

A sharp gust tugs my jerkin,
spreads it like a membrane,
me the bones within,
urges me to billow and like
Icarus, da Vinci, Bat-man,
I feel my feet go light.

For such a moment's transport,
a lasting image of recoil, the stuff
of nightmares. I grasp the fort
and coorie down into the lee,
and make towards the field to put
the fence between my dreams and me.

DIMINUENDO

Accordions are my pet hate,
distending their shapeless rubber balls
of sound, chording each single note
like a diamond in cotton wool:
I much prefer a flute

or the raucous blast that rips
the air from that stag in rut,
there, trumpeting from that hilltop,
his antlers sharp against the sky,
points clustered in spiked arpeggios
puncturing the blue rotundity,
snagging the clouds, daring those
who crowd him on his territory.

Beneath him the hill deflates
in furrowed ridges etched like staves
by the seeping moisture and the weight
of time. The stag roars above,
a moment clear, then muffled
in the slow chord of the sinking hills.

MOORLAND ALCHEMY

This Cheviot landscape once compared
to a herd of slaughtered horses bares
its naked flanks to the sky, skin
of blaeberry, ling and cotton grass, in
attitudes of blank submission.
Here soaring peaks are no distraction.

Winter dulls all sense of line;
snow cushions the heavy clouds;
fence wires honed to blades of ice
harvest the wind, their posts
become crustaceans shelled in rime —
the exoskeleton of winter.

Once, in Cheviot's western groin
we raised a fox couched among cairns
of avalanched ice. Contouring the hill
it rode surfer-like beneath the cornice wall,
smouldered a moment like the sun blood-red,
then set below the plateau's rim and disappeared.

Stark symmetry of tone and line,
afterimage on the retina, singes of urine
on snow, foot behind foot the curving spoor
shortest way between points: this creature
more than predator scavenging for kills,
and so much more than carrion these hills.

Martin Marroni

DONALD S. MURRAY

THE COMING OF ENGLISH

On the first Thursday in November, a telegram arrived at Chrissie's home.

Using her thumb-nail as a knife, she tore its envelope open and took the piece of paper out. She did not try to read the words that were written there. They were printed in English, a language she had never been taught. For a short time she stared at them, impressed by their mystery and cursed the lack of knowledge which prevented her from understanding the meaning of its words. Finally, she folded it away and placed it behind the tilly-lamp on the dresser. She would have to ask the local headmaster to read it to her later.

In the meantime, she decided to forget about it, pretending to herself it had never been received. There was work to be done. The sheep still had to be fed. The cow remained to be milked and cared for. Her son had gone away to the war which had recently started and the whole burden of the croft rested on her shoulders. Yet she never wasted any time complaining about this. She gave her work more attention and energy than she would ever have expected from anybody else.

When she had finally completed all the tasks she had set herself to do, she picked up the telegram in her hand and set off in the direction of the schoolhouse. There were others in the village who could read and understand English but she would always take any letter she received along to the headmaster. There was a coldness and distance about him which was lacking in her fellow villagers. With them, she could never be certain that her information would not be spread about the district, speeded by their quick and gossiping tongues. As she hurried along, she crumpled the envelope between her fingers, believing it contained some welcome news about her son.

She knocked at the schoolhouse door, granting it a respect she never gave to any other house in the district. For a few moments, she stood anxiously on the door-step. It was then the headmaster appeared. He was a grim-featured man, not given to warmth but his dark face lightened when he saw her.

'Good day, Chrissie. It's good to see you ... How are you keeping these days?'

'I'm fine, headmaster ... and you?'

'Grand.' He smiled in reply, gesturing to the open door. She followed him in, the warm scent of peat-fire filling her lungs as she entered the sitting-room. She always felt slightly awkward while she was there. The headmaster's wife kept a beautiful home. Its fine leather chairs glinted in the firelight. There were books stretched across one wall. She glanced at one that lay open on the fireside table, blind to the meaning of its words. The whole place seemed a world away from the darkness and damp of her own thatched cottage.

'Would you like a cup of tea?' the headmaster smiled.

'No ..., no.' she answered, waving her hand to emphasise her refusal. 'I just came along to ask you to read this for me.'

She held out the crumpled envelope between her fingers. The headmaster took it from her, withdrawing the piece of paper from its folds. He smiled cheerfully.

'It's a telegram.' he said.

The headmaster began to read it. As his eyes moved along the line, his face darkened, filling up with fear and doubt. He looked at her with sadness in his eyes.

'Sit down, Chrissie.' he said.

She obeyed him slowly, struggling to read his thoughts from his voice. The headmaster smoothed a hair back from his forehead.

'Your son's been killed.'

She said nothing, staring at the fire before her. He took his hankerchief from his pocket and wiped his brow. He was unsure whether or not his words had been understood.

'I'm sorry ... but John won't be returning from the war.'

Death is always strange. She remembered the day her husband had died. When the last sound had escaped him, she had continued to search his long familiar face for signs of life, swearing she could feel the warmth of his breath on her fingers. It seemed stranger still today. Trapped on a piece of paper, written in an unknown foreign tongue, it was somehow less real than it might otherwise have been. She shook her head and turned angrily towards the headmaster.

'Is that the way they tell people? A piece of paper ... A language that few here can understand ... Is that how they tell a mother that her son is dead?'

The headmaster shrugged his shoulders hopelessly, searching for the right reply.

She stood up. As she did so, a single tear fell down her cheek. She brushed it away angrily with the back of her hand. She would not cry here. In a room full of English books, her mourning would seem odd and out of place. Instead, she would return home. Her tears would fall there freely, untroubled by the language which had come to bring her death.

Donald S. Murray

AONGHAS MACNEACAIL

dol dhachaidh	going home
seall na geòidh a siubhal 's na gobhlaingaoithe	see the geese journeying and the swallows
's fhad/'o dh' fhalbh a' chubhag	long/since the cuckoo went
seall na duilleagan dearg ag éiridh air sgìath sgairtghaoith ag éiridh 's a siubhal	see the red leaves rising on the wing of a gust rising and travelling
tha 'm bradan sgriob mhór amach air a shlighe	the salmon is a great way out on his journey

ghrian a dol na sìneadh
ghealach ag éiridh
    'nam parabolan caochlaideach eòlach
	the sun reclining
	moon rising
	    in their familiar changing parabolas

samhradh a siubhal
fodhar air a dhruim
    cleòc mór a sgaoileadh as a dhéidh
	summer journeying
	autumn on his back
	    a great cloak spreading behind

null 's a nall air cala
    fogarrach a null 's a nall
null 's a nall
    null 's a nall
	back and forward on the wharf
	    an exile back and forward
	back and forward
	    back and forward

AONGHAS MACNEACAIL

RAGE AGAINST THE DYING OF

My first few weeks at school were devoted exclusively to learning a foreign language. Once my classmates and I had attained a sufficient degree of fluency in the imposed tongue our own language was discarded from the learning process.

The transition must have been effective and, superficially at least, painless, for no Gael I know can recollect the process. I certainly cannot. Our experience could not have been entirely without trauma, however. Just when we were most alert for the naming of things, including the common place which surrounded us, the language which should have been our natural tool — shared with peer-group and parents alike — was undermined by school. I quickly took it for granted that a little white flower which abounds in pasture and meadow is the daisy. I have to remind myself that it is also, and for me primarily, *neòinean.*

Naming things was not something which troubled my childhood. It was only when I began to write that naming became a matter of importance and, in the case of my native language, a source of frustration. If I have to think twice before identifying a common flower, there are more complex subjects, for which a rich vocabulary was once available, that are now, for my generation of Gaels, a burden to articulate. The necessary words have to be searched for in a range of inadequate, frequently antiquated, dictionaries. As often as not, the word stays unfound. It is accepted that the years of schooling, through to diplomass, degrees and doctorates, are the 'formative' years, during which the basic adult vocabulary is developed. For the Gael, as Gael, they have proved to be the deformative years. There is an entire lexical geography between the exotic and everyday, a whole range of concepts which are first named through the language of our schooling. In large areas of awareness, our native language has become, in effect, our second language.

The experience I have sketchily summarised in these few paragraghs is that of a generation of Gaels (the last) whose infancy predated the transistor age. With no television and hardly any radio available to influence our pre-literate minds, the impact of other languages on our lives was minimal: until school sucked us in and sought to suck the Gaelic out of us. It's much worse now. It's bound to be, given that television is available to every Gaelic household at the flick of a switch: and television only speaks Gaelic on extremely rare occasions. As the parents of today's infants belong to the very generation that school did so much to degaelicise, it's small wonder if they should lack the will or confidence to assert their native tongue in the face of such a persuasive influence.

The tragedy of the Gaelic experience in this century is that what should have enriched our lives — the acquisition of a second language — was actually a means of alienation and impoverishment. It is essential to consider such facts in any assessment of the role, or place, of the Gaelic writer in contemporary society. In reflecting on our circumstances, I find myself surprised that I, or any of my generation of Gaels should have chosen to write in our native language at all.

Gaelic authors of earlier generations were less beset by such dilemmas. Those whose childhood predated the 1872 Education Act (which established compulsory education throughout Scotland yet omitted to acknowledge the existence of the Gaelic language) lived their lives relatively untouched by any other language. As often as not they were non-literate — a very different thing from being illiterate except in the specific sense of being unable to read. For them the mind was word-store as well as word-mill. In their relatively self contained world they could happily be, and frequently were, monoglot.

Even those who moved out of their native territories, into the lowland cities, could submerge themselves in communities of their own people. As early as the 1790's, the noted bard Duncan Ban MacIntyre served in an Edinburgh City Guard that was almost entirely composed of Highlanders.

In the late 19th Century, Mary MacPherson, Skye-born laureate of the Highland Land Law Reform movement, spent ten years in Glasgow, As she trained, and worked, as a midwife and district nurse on Clydeside, she could hardly have been monoglot. We may safely assume, however, that the essential world for her and her generation, as for many Highlanders after them, was the world of their fellow expatriate Gaels. There were Gaelic churches and Gaelic concert-houses which nourished, in very different ways, the spirit of the urban Gaelic communities. The commitment of 'Great Mary of the Songs' to the land campaign was also an essentially Gaelic matter. The society most threatened by lawless landlordism was that of her own people, the predominantly Gaelic crofters in the North and West. Whatever problems they may have had to overcome, both Donnchadh Bàn and Màiri Mhór would have remained innocent of the dilemma which confronts their twentieth century counterparts. Both were steeped in their own culture. Each had a virtuosic command of the language. They knew, without presumption, that an audience existed which could comprehend their work.

We, their literary descendants, enjoy no such luxury. We cannot put words to metre or pen to paper without having made a choice. Having resolved our first dilemma — whether Gaelic is any longer a legitimate vehicle — we still have to assess the particular circumstances and ask, *which language do I use?* It's not simply a matter of mood, style or etiquette like *what suit should I wear?* Even if we 'are what we eat' I don't believe that substituting the subtleties of French or Indian cuisine for the homelier bannocks, beef stew or brose would have a profound effect on our psyche. With language there is something much deeper at stake. The language I elect, or am required, to use is not only a means of self expression, it is the elemental medium through which I connect with the society I inhabit.

Assuming I have a need to make contact with that society, a number of issues must be resolved. They include

(1) Which layer of the demographic onion do I mean when I say 'the society I inhabit'? Am I referring to the relatively homogeneous parish or to the gallimaufrous nation?
(2) Will my message be intelligible to that society?
(3) Is that society likely to be interested in what I have to say?

One reasonable answer to the first question is that, even without aspiring to the universal, I can, and do inhabit more than one society, or subculture. If, within Scotland, I am addressing the community of writers, I will adopt a different register from the one I use with my fellow Gael. Not only will the register I use be different, it will also be nesessary for me to use a different language, as only a tiny proportion of my fellow-writers share the Gaelic language with me.

But supposing Gaelic is the only language I want to use? It is, after all, my first language, mother tongue, natural language: it is the language in which I first articulated such elemental feelings as love, hunger, fear. Why should it not also be the language in which I articulate the more sophisticated concerns of my maturity? Why not, indeed, except that if I take myself seriously as a writer — if I see writing as being my primary occupation, not just a preoccupation — I have to recognise that I live in a materialistic world. The work I produce, be it poetry, prose or drama, has to command a market.

What audience, then, am I likely to have? According to the 1981 census, less than 80,000 Gaelic-speakers remain alive in Scotland. There may be a scattering elsewhere, with odd concentrations like the ageing Gaelic community in Cape Breton Island, but the essential Gaelic society, which must concern me, is represented by that four score thousand who inhabit the traditional homeland. Of their number, the great majority will be, for reasons already alluded to, illiterate in their own language. The minority which remains, which is not in the strictest sense illiterate, must itself be further subdivided. There is every reason to believe that a large proportion of Gaels who *can* read would regard themselves as only partially literate. These would certainly be unable to write in their own language. Many acquired what reading skills they do have not at school but from the churches. Sunday schools, Bible-classes and particularly the parallel-text New Testament have helped many Gaels toward literacy in their native tongue. Nevertheless, many who can read substantial chapters of the Bible with confidence will baulk at a short piece written in their own colloquial speech patterns. (Biblical Gaelic, a synthetic form dating from the 18th Century, is the nearest we have to a 'Standard Gaelic'. It is not, however, normally heard outwith the devotional environment.)

We still have to find our competent, confident Gaelic general reader. Those who fit the description are likely to have studied Gaelic throughout their secondary schooling, and probably beyond. As a proportion of the eighty thousand, they represent only a fragment. Even if we isolate this fragment, numbering no more than a couple of thousand *at most,* as the total potential readership a Gaelic writer may expect to command, we must accept that such a readership will be no more homogeneous than any other reading public. Gaelic literary tastes like those of other societies, run the gamut from Peoples' Friend to Pound or Pliny. In such circumstances, the most popular Gaelic author will quickly recognise that writing solely in the native language is not a commercially viable venture. It's as well that Gaelic writers are not primarily motivated by the size of the potential audience, nor by the likelihood of any significant financial benefit accruing from their labours.

It is, though, a cause for anger that such a situation should exist, not so much from the point of view of the writer but from that of the reader. If, say, only ten out of 80,000, or 80 million for that matter, should want to read my work, then I must look to the quality, or relevance of my work. But if only a small multiple of tens out of the eighty thousand *can* read the work of any Gaelic writer, it is clear that something is seriously amiss, particularly as we inhabit a culture that takes pride in its level of adult literacy. There are historical causes, of course. I've already made passing reference to the Education Act of 1872, which achieved in Law what successive regimes since that of the most foolish sage Jamie the Saxt had sought to obtain through legislation — the extirpation of the 'savage Irishe tongue'. Fortunately, *de facto* ignored *de jure,* and the language survives, if debilitated by its long struggle to stage a successful educational resurrection. The struggle continues.It is essentially, the struggle for the survival of the language itself.

In the days when the world of the Gael was a Gaelic world and education — the acquisition of knowledge — an osmotic part of being, the survival of the language and its rich literary treasury could be taken for granted. The question did not, could not, even arise. There have been many changes since then. For a long time now, Gaelic in the Gaelic community has been peripheral to the educational process. It has been squeezed into an equally marginal role in other fields where the larger world impinges on that of the Gael. I should not be considered paranoid if I assert that there are powerful and malign influences who begrudge it even that precarious peripheral existence. Such influences are powerful because of the positions they occupy, either as 'elected representatives' or as high-ranking operatives within the bureaucracies, both national and local. They are malign not so much because of what they do but because of what they contrive to avoid doing. For them, the continuing survival of Gaelic is an irritant. God knows why, but it is. The concept of a Gaelic Revival is, to them, an idea charged with negative energy as welcome as an unprotected radio-active isotope. It has to be contained neutralised, isolated, so that it cannot energise others. If kept dormant for long enough, it will turn to lead. It will have lost its disseminative potency while still retaining the capacity to poison.

The black militia engaged in this campaign operates as I have suggested, at various levels of the body politick. Sometimes they act clandestinely. As often as not they are quite brazen. Their ranks include Ordinance Survey cartographers who for perfectly logical reasons find it impossible to restore Gaelic placenames to their proper form and status. These deprive us of a geography. They include Governement stationers who are unable to provide us with official forms or documents in our own language. (This is a way of saying that Government does not recognise our right, as a community, to exist, however platitudinously politicians may appear to plead the contrary.) They include broadcasting administrators, some of whom have acquired our language. They may wish us well, but they do not feel that they can promise ever to be able to provide is with a comprehensive broadcasting service in Gaelic. Such a response makes them also tacit conspirators in the scheme to elimate us. They will also be found running schools, colleges, universities and departments of education.

They may and, frequently do, overflow with goodwill, but each will have an excuse. No matter how much they wish to help, there will be convincing reasons why they cannot do anything to further the development of the language or culture of the Gaels. Even when the expression 'further the development' means no more than 'attempt to sustain the existence', these bland cultural assassins will use the force of their own inaction to tighten the noose around the already emaciated neck of our Gaelic heritage. It is as well for the British Establishment that such people are its allies, not its enemies. They may seem the least probable candidates for membership of a guerilla force, but there is no denying their effectiveness. Almost without exception, they present themselves as pillars of society, the class of people who most eminently qualify for the designation 'reasonable'. There could be no better cover for a hit-squad. And how ineffably reasonable they appear to be when they deploy the most shattering weapon in their armoury. This projectile, small but significant, is the verbal equivalent to a nuclear hand-grenade. It is the innocuously disjunctive conjunction *but*.

'We'd like to, *but* ...' How often have we heard, the sympathy disarming — then the devastation. In a recent superb example of the genre, a spokesman for the Consultative Committee on the Curriculum pronounced the CCC in 'sympathy with the aspirations of' its own Committee on Gaelic, 'so far as these are commensurate with the availability of resources.' The absence of a naked 'but' does not prove me wrong: the quotation is suffused with the essence of butness. Of course, the butlers of destruction have been with us for a long time. They will probably always be with us.

This essay set out to explore the place of a Gaelic writer in the community. In that context, its worth acknowledging that Willie Neill, in the last issue of *Chapman*, correctly identified yet another cell of destroyers. They are the analysts and anthologists of Scottish Literature who glibly excuse themselves for omitting anything on, or in, Gaelic, while continuing to serve up their product as a legitimate representation of *Scottish* writing. Gaelic writers, like all fellow Gaels, inhabit a precarious, inconstant, instrinsically hostile world. Sometimes there is good earth underneath their feet, sometimes hard stone. Then when they least expect it, there is vacancy. All the landmarks they might expect to recognise spin out of focus, and out of sight. Successive generations who suffered the same dislocation as I did at the age of five will be familiar with the experience. And still we continue to ride such storms. And still, somehow, we survive. We survived James the Sixth, for all his Bills and Statutes. We survived the educational exterminators of 1872. We expect, and receive, no support from their successors, but we endure.

Twentieth Century Gaeldom may seem to be teetering on the brink. It has, nevertheless, produced, in Sorley MacLean arguably the greatest Gaelic poet of all time, and a figure of richly-deserved international standing in our own time. During his career as a schoolmaster, MacLean felt compelled to engage much of his own precious time and energy in resisting the tides of cultural genocide. He became particularly, for a time obsessively, involved during his headship of Plockton Secondary School. Each annual intake of pupils was further evidence that Gaelic was dying on its feet in one of its former heartlands, Wester Ross. MacLean, with others, chose to campaign for the introduction of a *Learners* Higher Grade paper in Gaelic. Inevitably, they met stiff resistance from the coharts of crassness, but they fought on, and won. They won that crucial battle, but MacLean would be first to recognise that the struggle for Gaelic in education is far from over. Despite the bilingual programmes and projects that have followed in its wake, the struggle is very far from over.

In retrospect, it seems more than a little ridiculous that MacLean and his friends should have had to fight at all. What they were asking for, in reality, was no more than equal status for Gaelic with other modern languages such as French, German or Russian. Till then, it had existed in a kind of educational ghetto, taught as if it *were* a foreign language, yet at such a standard as to be accessible only to the most academically able native speakers. Now we have a syllabus for learners. In theory it should be possible for any secondary pupil in Scotland to study Gaelic. The 'butlers' make damn sure it won't be.

For almost two decades, Sorley MacLean published virtually nothing. During that time he wrote no poetry. Teaching, particularly the teaching of his own language and culture, concerned him deeply. At the end of his working day, there would have been precious little energy left for poetry. We may regret the limitation this imposed on the corpus of MacLean's poetry. He cannot be regarded as any the less a poet for it. MacLean himself would consider it imperative that the poet should be involved in the issues of the day, particularly as they affect the society he belongs to. Those of us who are Gaels and writers are unlikely to forget that we are Gaels first and that the society we, primarily, belong to is that remnant of Gaeldom which, by some peculiar miracle, survives.

Still we cannot take for granted that the language we use in any given circumstances will be our own. As writers we have to make a conscious choice to use Gaelic. Such a decision may exclude the great majority of our fellow Gaels from immediate access to our work. It also excludes us, the writers from the responses of that portion of our fellow Gaels. These awarenesses, paradoxically, strengthen my conviction that choosing our native language to express our deepest thoughts is a necessary, political, act.

gleann fadamach	glen remote
pléin a dol tarsuing cho àrd 's nach cluinnear i long a dol sìos an cuan ach fada mach air fàire	plane crossing so high it can't be heard ship going down the ocean far out on the horizon
cuid dhe 'n t-saoghal a siubhal 's a siubhal	a part of the world travelling travelling
's a bhaile seo chan eileas a siubhal ach an aon uair 's na clachan a rinn ballaichean a dol nan càirn	in this village people only travel once and the stones that made walls become cairns

Aonghas MacNeacail

AONGHAS MACNEACAIL

from sireadh bradain sicir

2. nuair a bha mi
   san t-saoghal roimhe
   sheinn do thuinn duan
   air m'fhorradhruim gun tàmh

   bha mi nam iasgair
   bha mi nam shealgair
   na d'shaoghal riaslach
   thar bharr nam tonn

   thigeadh grian gu tràigh
   gealach gu treabhadh
   crodh cuain gam buachailleachd
   gu buaile lìonach

4. aig bristeadh là
   na h-uairean
   dol nan spruilleach

   mi nam shealgair

   an uamh nan reul
   gun ghlaodhaich treubh
      is sinne clann a bhoghafrois
      fo chairt no bian no ite
      sinn
      do bhràithrean is do pheathraichean

   is dh'éirich seabhag bho mo làimh
   air thòir an ùirsgéil
   (naidheachd air a bhradan eagnaidh)

   sheas damh air faire
   an dubhair doire

5. *bha mi nam iasgair*

   sìos
   fromh 'n fhuaran shuaineach sìos
   an taisdealach tromh
   theine 's fline sìos
   air thòir a bhradain sìos
   ri solus coinnle sìos
   gu ruige crìdh na linne

   faic do chaoraich
   trom air lian
   gun fhaireachadh air sgian

   stiùir do bhuar
   'o mhol an staimh

   Thig gaillionn
   sneachd thar bharr nam beannaibh
   eader na féidh is an fiarach
   an gaillionn thar uile
   gach iasg air faondradh

seeking wise salmon

2. when i was
   in the former world
   your waves unceasingly
   drew music from my keel

   i was a fisher
   i was a hunter
   in your sundering world
   above the waves

   sun come to shore
   moon to ploughing
   sea-cattle herded
   to net-filled fold

4. at break of day
   the hours
   disintegrating

   i was a hunter

   in the cave of stars
   a tribe proclaimed
      we are the rainbow's children
      barked, or furred or feathered
      we
      your brothers and your sisters

   and a hawk rose from my hand
   to hunt the fable
   (news of the wise salmon)

   a stag stood sentry
   in dark of copse

5. *i was a fisher*

   down
   through the winding fountain down
   the traveller through
   fire and sleet still down
   in search of salmon down
   by candleflicker down
   to reach the heart of the pool

   see your sheep
   pregnant on meadows
   unconscious of knives

   steer your cattle
   from sea-tangle beach

   storm will come
   snow deeper than the high peaks
   between the deer and their grazing
   storm over all
   world's fish astray

madaidhean coille
gun tamh gun chadal
dreathan gun fhasgadh

forest wolves
without rest or sleep
wren without shelter

bha mi nam dhuin air
talamh cruaidh
a dùbhlan fàsaich
a sireadh bhradain
(tromh thobar tiompain)

i was a man
upon the land
defying wilderness
in search of salmon
(through a drumming well)

nuair a bha mi
'san t-saoghal eile
bhuail do bhódhran
orm ruithim shìnteach

when i was
in the other world
your bodhran beat
on me a striding rhythm

9. là an taghaidh
   dh' iadh thu mi
   na d'ghlac
   na d'chuairtshruth

9. on the day of choosing
   you took me
   into your embrace
   your whirlpool

an coilltean oidhche
faghaid gun tàmh
madadh mialchu
damhan beach air
thòir ceann-uidhe

in the woods of night
a ceaseless stalking
wolf and deerhound
spider bee
pursue objective

danns am fàinn an
ruidhle torraich
cnò ruadh calltuinn
air do bhilean

dance in the ring of
the reel of plenty
red hazel kernel
on your lips

cròg dhonn air teud
s tu seinn do naidheachd
air stalcair eàlaidh
an cumadh bradain

brown paw on harpstring
as you sing your tale
of that elusive sleuth
disguised as salmon

san t-saoghal roimhe
coinnean sa ghealaich
a maistreadh cungaidh
dha 'n t-sealgair chreuchde
a thàrr an iomairt

in the former world
rabbit in the moon
mixed remedies
for wounded hunters
who endured the struggle

san t-saoghal roimhe
muilt gan rùsgadh
ri sultghaoth samhraidh
bradain a sgiathadh eas
a teicheadh breunloch
nam bruadar deòghann
san t-saoghal eile
   shir mi shir mi
   am bradan sicir
   sear air ghealaich
   siar air reultan
shir is fhuair mi
fhuair mi sealladh

in the former world
wethers are sheared
in summer-fat breeze
salmon wing rapids
fleeing slack pools
of faint-life dreams
in the other world
   i hunted for
   the salmon of wisdom
   east of moon
   west of stars
i searched and caught
i caught a glimpse

Aonghas Macneacail

WALTER PERRIE

CALLING (OUT) MACDIARMID

' ... Explanations come to an end somewhere.' *Wittgenstein:*
(Philosophical Investigations)

To call (something) out is not (necessarily or exactly) the same as to cry (it) out, though they may coincide. To explore and elucidate what is involved in calling (something out as a something) is, I take it, one of Wittgenstein's primary concerns in the *Investigations*. For a calling to be grammatical it has to satisfy those criteria which determine (are used to determine) correct usage. What will *count as* correct usage will be what is agreed to satisfy agreed criteria — a grammer. To call something (something) is *at least* to call it (to and for ourselves) out. A call is eloquent of the grammer of the form of life in which it must be embedded. It makes (has) no sense apart from its form of life and only happens when prompted by some want in our form of living. And any calling out, as an expression of a want, is thereby an admission. It is to admit to (enroll in) our community of hopes and fears another (or the same?) confession?

When I read a poem by MacDiarmid I am made aware that there is something odd or unusual about reading a poem 'by MacDiarmid' in a way there isn't about reading a poem by Yeats or Rilke. I know perfectly well that *Hugh MacDiarmid* was one of the several pen-names used by Christopher Murray Grieve. Could anyone want to say that a poem was composed by a name? Perhaps the matter should rest there and we should simply say that the poem was composed by C.M. Grieve and published under the pen-name *Hugh MacDiarmid.* But I am uneasy about that simple saying; sense that it misses something. After all, if someone were to tell me that he had been reading a poem by MacDiarmid and I said: *you mean by C.M. Grieve,* he could quite reasonably say that that's not what he meant at all. Not every poem by C.M. Grieve is also a poem by Hugh MacDiarmid (or Hugh M'Diarmid). There are probably lots of people who have read a poem by C.M. Grieve, published as a poem by Hugh MacDiarmid, without ever being aware that *Hugh MacDiarmid* was a pen-name of C.M. Grieve.

Perhaps it seems unreasonable to insist on the distinction too much but that would suggest that we could be sure of what the distinction really meant. To refuse to recognise it fully (call it out) is a way of claiming that it's not important. And yet, it was evidently important enough to Grieve for him to go on using it long after the fact that *Hugh MacDiarmid* was one of his pen-names was public knowledge — at least to his immediate literary audience in Scotland. It seems unreasonable, though not impossible, to insist that Grieve's continued use of *MacDiarmid* was perverse or was just a habit that stayed because it liked him. It invites the question: how do you know?

I want to say that the name (MacDiarmid) *is* important: that in some respect it is to be read as part of (or as a clue to the reading of) the poem. Does it stand in relation to the poem as parentheses to parts of formulae in formal logic, that is; marks the poem off by calling (inducing the reader to call) it a 'MacDiarmid poem'? Perhaps it (the name) operates more after the fashion of the preamble to a contract. Contracts are parts of (elements in) some larger enterprise though parts, perhaps, of a peculiarly decisive kind: they lay down the rules (procedures, expectations?) for (some) subsequent operations. We do not enter into contracts without a reason for so doing.

I know from some of his early letters (to George Ogilvie) that from at least his late teens Christopher Grieve claimed (called out? admitted to?) a sense of some overwhelming personal destiny which was articulated with (or in relation to) his — for want of a more precise phrase — vision of Scotland as a place and people. I know too that *MacDiarmid* derives from (what translates into English as) *son of Diarmid* and that Diarmid was a hero of the pre-Christian Celtic sagas who, like all such heroes, was entangled in an overwhelming personal (and tribal) destiny — overwhelming to the point of death. Perhaps then it is not unreasonable further to translate *MacDiarmid* as *son of a destined man.* Not every poem by Grieve was so-bracketed. Why did Grieve so-bracket some and, as it turned out, most of his poems? Was there some pressing practical reason or was there (instead or also) some other *kind* of reason: to encourage the destiny, to make it objective? He did bracket the poems in question. Is bracketing here the sort of gesture to be read as: when I do *this,* I want it to be understood *thus* ...; and why would Grieve want it so? *Why* questions can be answered from (at least) two perspectives. We can begin by saying *Because* and go on to state a series of conditions which produced the event. Or we can begin by saying *In order that* and go on to state motives or intentions relating to a desired result or effect.

Poems call (for something from) their performers. Is what each poem calls out (for) specific to each poem or to each performer? How is it that we know (do we know?) what any particular poem calls for? What makes us believe that it's a poem at all? Because it's in a book of poems? Because the author and publisher assert that it's a book of poems? Because poems have certain characteristics or qualities peculiar to poems? *This* table has four legs. Some tables have three (or two) legs. Are there legless tables? When is a table (at what point is it) damaged beyond being a table? As Wittgenstein remarks: 'What has to be accepted, the given, is — so one could say — *forms of life.' (Investigations)* A table is not a table when an entire speech-community (culture?) is agreed that *it* is not a table — refuses to call out 'table'.

Suppose a poet to say: what I give you in *this* is a poem. If the culture says: No, *it* (that) is not a poem, or; We refuse to call *that* (out as) a poem, (refuse to respond in a poem-responsive way) has *it* lost its poemness? And why might a community refuse to respond in the poet-wanted way? Why might agreement break down to such an extent? Is it that what is required is intolerable — unbearable for a whole community — so that it must exorcise itself? What would knowing the answer be like? Like knowing a form of life which is also to become aware of its limits? What would be required in order to know the grammer of 'by MacDiarmid'?

But the jury has been packed — the outcome rigged — for I began with 'Suppose a poet to say ...' The imagined breakdown would probably not, in this instance, extend so far into desperation. In this case poet and community might go back to first principles to heal the breach beacuse the community *has already accepted* that a *poet* is in question. It might, therefore, recognise 'special skills' or 'wider experience of poetry'. Perhaps poet and interlocutors can *go back* and agree: *this* and *this* and *this* are poems. And the poet can then explain how what he (or she) has offered bears on *this* and *this* and *this.* Or, more likely, someone will explain for him (or her) with one of those charming ritual addresses which must begin: 'The poet ...' But there are other perspectives from which to view such breakdowns. Perhaps the interlocutors *mean* (grammatically?): We are prepared to reveal ourselves in *such* and *such* and *such* responses, to confess so much but no more, beyond that, what you ask is unacceptable, intolerable, unbearable. Is that how it may be seen by a *young* person, or by a schizophrenic? Is it, as Wittgenstein says: 'The fundamental fact here is that we lay down rules, a technique, for a game, and that then when we follow the rules, things do not turn out as we had assumed. That we are therefore as it were entangled in our own rules.' *(Investigations.)* Is there for each culture a grammer of its limits?

What is called out if I recite: By Hugh MacDiarmid —

EMPTY VESSEL

I met ayont the cairney
A lass wi' tousie hair

Singin' till a bairnie
That was nae langer there.

Wunds wi' warlds to swing
Dinna sing sae sweet,
The licht that bends owre a' thing
Is less ta'en up wi't.

To call (out) is to draw attention to, to attend to and summon. What calls us so? The performer places (locates) *himself* (or *herself*) before the calling. The bored schoolchild compelled to read a MacDiarmid poem cannot be compelled to call it before him or herself: cannot confess before it. The best that he or she can genuinely do is to acknowledge the coercion and go on from there. To put oneself truly before the poem can only be a free act but free because we want it and not because there is no reason to.

Forms of life can be variously fluid but not so much that they have no grammar. Such living — without a grammar — is unimaginable. The rules of a game can be changed piecemeal. New games can be invented. How could one play a-game-without-rules? What is tricky in any particular case is seeing what will constitute and *adequate* translation (formulation, extraction) of a grammar. The notion of adequacy requires us to ask: adequate for what? A good way to begin is to look at who is using (applying, flexing) the grammer, where and when and within which (historical) form of life. Only then can a (possible) motive become intelligible.

Flexing the rules (or the wrong rules) at the wrong time can be dangerous — even fatal. How might one go about characterising the writings of (say) Lewis Carroll, J.L. Borges, Mandelstam, Beckett, on the basis of the grammer of their biographies? Perhaps *knowing that* (genuinely knowing and not just failing to make sense) is always translatable into *knowing how to under specific conditions.*

Within this culture (European, British, Scottish?) what moves a human being to make poems not as a hobby but as a life-and-death struggle (for) destiny? That it should be unmotivated is not even properly sayable. In Grieve's case immediate financial reward and material well-being are hardly in question. The sort of neurotic-compulsion account offered by Ann Boutelle in *Thistle and Rose* is dishonest because it pretends to be about explaining the poems but takes as its major premise the unreality of the poems *as poems.* Her theories shear off at crazy angles away from the poems. She denies (refuses) that the poem can call her out at all — refuses to confess that they are poems while claiming to explain them. It is like the case of the sick man and his visitor. The sick man says — *hold my hand* and the visitor, backing away, replies — *it's the pain that causes it.*

What kind of sense does it make to say that a (someone's) motive is impersonal? In Grieve's case the motive must be, structurally, related to the poems, thereby, to their calling out. If, for a moment, we put to one side all the difficulties about the relationship(s) between Hugh MacDiarmid and C.M. Grieve, can we try to put the poem before us? I imagine myself to meet a friend (or complete stranger) on the street while I'm out shopping. Or I'm out for a walk in some country place and meet a friend (or complete stranger). Or I go to visit a friend in hospital. In any (or each) case the person says to me *and* says genuinely *and* I am not thinking about poems at all: I met ayont the cairney a lass wi tousie hair, singin' till a bairnie that was nae langer there. Wunds wi warlds to swing dinna sing sae sweet, the licht that bends owre a' thing is less ta'en up wi't.

But he *(or she)* wouldn't (couldn't) *just* say it. How would (could) it be said and what sort of response would the saying solicit? Pity — fear — anger — love? How could (would) I react in such a situation? Why would the stranger (or friend) say it to *us*? Why *say* it to us? The moment registered by a genuine saying of the words has to be extreme — *in extremis.* The words in such a saying are of a want, of pity, love, wonder

— the tragedy. Unless, of course, we *choose* to invent a context which will castrate them, trivialise them, and we can do so only by making an effort to do so. It is the kind of moment when our naked frailties are revealed, when poor, unaccommodated man faces the storm, wonders how to cope, looks for help, confesses his helplessness.

What are we to *do* when a friend, or a stranger suddenly become a friend, or a friend suddenly become a stranger, calls us out so and so confesses? An aesthetic appreciation of the situation *might* be (part of) a response. People are complicated. But would we not want to say that that would be backing-off: would be irresponsible, or a more tragic kind of confession than helplessness?

But, after all, it's only a poem. Something gets said (called out) when there is an issue — something unresolved — something at stake — a problem of difficulty — a need to say, even if the saying is chatter. What do we *do* when we confront ourselves — freely — with a work such as 'Empty Vessel'?: when we make ourselves available to being called out so? Who confronts us? The author may be dead. In any case, never appears as poem. And the poem never exists *as such* — only as marks on paper — until we summon it before us — place our selves before its questioning. How much of *aesthetic* experience is a cover-up for our intolerable frailties or a half-made acknowledgement or a vicious backin-off?

When I remember (put together again) some of those episodes in my own history (biography) in which such helplessness has *had* to be acknowledged or in which (in retrospect) I confess a failure of acknowledgement, the patterns of anxiety and distress which have been characteristic of those episodes have been clearly bracketed by the episodes themselves. Another way of putting it is to say that they are exceptional experiences or peak moments: crystallisations of (other) biographical trends. The very fact that such episodes are episodes or crises underlines their bracketed nature.

How often has one heard it said after some upheaval in someone's life — after a death or some similarly difficult confrontation — words to the effect that: *Life must go on.* It is not so much that life must go on but that, being embedded as we are in determinate forms of life, life *will* go on, in any case. And how often too do such expressions signal an avoidance. The crisis or peak episode requires us to confront our helplessness and to do something about it: to respond in some way to the fact that a form of life has shown itself (or been shown) to be in some respect inadequate. Or its grammar has been disrupted. In order to go on at all, agreement has to be re-established and that *can* only be done on the basis of prior, *de facto* agreements. Perhaps it is not required that all the parties go back to first principles. It would be difficult to imagine such a situation for the grammar is disrupted in differing degrees for different persons at different times. A wholesale disruption such as that which resulted in the revolution in 1917 in Russia has to have quite specific causes. What Sartre (not always successfully) is trying to get at is the fact that it is those crisis-episodes which bring to the surface the conventionality of a grammar.

Sartre believes that disruptions in our grammar make clear the possibilty of freedom. But it is difficult to know what such possibilty means. Sartre's argument is, in essence, that because it can (does) happen at a specific time, in a certain place, then it can be willed or made to happen *all* the time. That view is based on a very high level of abstraction from specificity. The point is not that such episodes do (and therefore can) happen, but that they happen under specific conditions: that they are precisely *breakdowns* in the agreements which (tacitly for most of the time) constitute or underpin forms of actual life. A form of life which consisted *only* of episodes when the rules were breached is a *logical* absurity, is not imaginable. It is not that life *can* go on (what does such a 'can' mean?) but that life *does* go on. That the breakdowns present themselves in Sartre's accounts as occurring for individuals individually (usually in isolation or one at a time) is a measure of the distance between Sartre and the historical materialism he claimed to have espoused. What I am suggesting is that it is a condition of such experiences happening at all that they be bracketed. The irremediable obscurity of some of Sartre's (and Heidegger's) writings on these topics is generated by his efforts to think away (or without) the brackets. One might draw a useful parallel here between Sartre's methodology and the nature of the Cartesian principle of systematic doubt and Husserl's phenomenological reduction. Both Sartre and Husserl think of freedom as an *abstract* state or condition rather than as the completely specific choices we make in daily life in which we, as it were, fiddle with the limits of action.

This excursus should have illuminated something of what I mean here by *bracketing* and *grammar*. To return to MacDiarmid: one of the extraordinary features of many of the lyrics in *Sangschaw* and *Penny Wheep* and in general situation in which the protagonist in the *Drunk Man* finds himself, is the *extremity* they present. Life, so to speak, within the poems, is ungrammatical except, of course, that some systematic grammer is a prerequisite of any poem at all.

A life-or-death struggle with (for) a destiny simply cannot be sustained *all the time* by anyone. The notion has no sense. It is difficult to struggle with destiny when the coal has to be fetched, the bed made or a meal prepared — not out of the question, but difficult. Grieve's poems (like anyone else's) were bracketed by (and within) his particular biography. But a view of poetry which holds that (part of) the business of poetry is a *peculiarly* public destiny (a destiny which entangles both personal fate and national development) *has* to be bracketed more firmly and clearly than is generally the case: otherwise, a sense of personal inadequacy generated by the mundane necessities of daily life will simply destroy the form of life in which the activity of making poems is embedded. A vision of destiny may be in (or of) a personal life, but it cannot *be* that life. Yeats, I think, had some similar point in mind when he insisted that the poet must not be confused with the man, with 'the bundle of accident and incoherence that sits down to breakfast ...'

MacDiarmid was not Grieve but Grieve's vision of the man of destiny *(son of a destined man)*, his *Zarathustra,* to labour an old theme. Nietzsche did struggle to submerge the daily round in the vision of destiny and Nietzsche's fate might be a timely warning to young men or romantics, though that, somehow, misses the point. Perhaps the more urgent point is that grammer does (and therefore can) change or be changed — in degrees, at times, in places, be *him* and *him* — and who else? And that grammatical shifts are impelled by wants in how we presently go on.

How we presently go on is what returns us to the missing element of our account (hitherto) or what happens when we place our selves before a MacDiarmid poem. The extent to (or frequency with) which we want or need to remove the brackets from a poem is a feature of each particular biography, will vary with time and circumstance. How often (or whether) we take away not just the brackets which read 'MacDiarmid' but those which read 'poem' — that so desirable safety-valve — we can only determine for ourselves. A full or total confrontation with certain poems may be as rare as the extremity the poem presents. The author's part in the business (Grieve's part) has been to present us with an artifact which can (will sometimes for some people) provoke or encourage (and structure?) a confrontation with the grammar of a life or a form of life, as it has been and (perhaps) as it will become. A continual process of adjustment in relation to other people is the necessary condition of possibility for any form of life. Art and life are not opposed or wholly distinct. The distinction arises from quite specific features of the grammar of a particular form of life.

The reasons (motives?) why someone confronts a poem are as various as life itself. The relevant point here is that each poem has a fixed structure (sequence.and content) so that the idea of a definite confrontation with a given poem is by no means wholly abstract for the confrontation must follow the sequence laid down by the author if it is to be a confrontation with *that* poem. What I want to suggest is that the extremity characteristic of some of the MacDiarmid lyrics and *A Drunk Man* (which is not, I think, dissimilar in degree to that of *Lear*) has a content which *all* such extreme situations share. I have stressed the ideas of *calling out* and *confession* because these expressions emphasise the *otherness* of what the individual confronts in extremity. If, at such moments, there is no-one to call out to, to confess to, then we are not so much helpless as destroyed. The point of calling-out a helplessness is to get help: to establish the *need* for a re-establishment of workable conventions, rules, agreements for a different (inevitably different) form of life.

Why have so many twentieth-century writers taken their own lives? Taken them where? It is, rather, taking *away* one's life and that *means* taking it away from a specific form of life — from certain times, places and persons when all the contracts have been torn up and the agreements are void or empty, when assent has been withdrawn. It has not, I think, been sufficiently noticed that emptiness is a dominant motif in the MacDiarmid poems — emptiness and ruin. Two things come irresistibly to mind. The first is by my friend, the Belgian poet, frank de crits (my translation from his Dutch and printed here by his courtesy):

TO COMMIT SUICIDE

only the sap-sucking blackfly survive
the boat of arthur craven the train of attila jozsef
the seine of paul celan the marne of leon deubel
the cocaine of georg trakl the heroin of roger-gilbert lecomte
the exhaust fumes of a car for dirk de witte and stig dagerman
the shotgun of ernest hemingway the pistol of drieu la rochelle
the opened wrist-veins and the hanging of sergei jessenin
the rope from the beam in the garret of jean-pierre duprey
the cord from the bars of a grating of gérard de nerval
the placard on the chest of rené crevel with the word: dégouté
the bitter hemlock of socrates the strychnia-seeds of mario de ça carneiro
the sleeping pills the alcohol the gas oven of ilarie voronca
the gas oven of sylvia plath the sleeping pills of cesare pavese
the alcohol of brendan dylan edgar and jack
the narrotics and barbiturates of raymond rouseel and gérald neveu
the huge dose of opium of jacques vaché with his two friends
the water of the sea of frans babylon the bullet in the heart of jacques rigaut
the water of the river virginia woolf the window onto the street for jan arends
the sunstroke of petrus borel the death-by-rats of thomas chatterton
only the sap-sucking blackfly survive.

The second is that extraordinary passage from the *Drunk Man* where the protagonist is addressing Dostoievski:

The wan leafs shak' atour us like the snaw,
Here is the cavaburd in which Earth's tint.
There's naebody but Oblivion and us,
Puir gangrel buddies wanderin' hameless in't.

The stars are larochs o' auld cottages,
And a' Time's glen is fu o' blinnin' stew.
Nae freen'ly lozen skimmers: and the wund
Rises and separates even me and you.

I ken nae Russian and you ken nae Scots.
We canna tell oor voices frae the wund.
The snaw is seekin' everywhere: oor herts
At last like roofless ingles it has f'und,

And gethers there in drift on endless drift,
Oor broken herts that it can never fill;
And still — its leafs like snaw, its growth like wund —
The thistle rises and forever will! ...

The (imaginary) protagonist in a poem by an (imaginary) person addresses a dead Russian novelist. And a catalogue of dead writers.

In the poet's extremity to *whom* is he to call (out) and who will (or can) answer? In this (our) form of life (in Europe now) too often (intolerably) the living poet's real community is, as Auden says: 'haphazardly scattered over the earth,' or, more often, *in* the earth, so that the community is imaginary — names and wishes and memories. And what is literature in such case but the confrontation of a self with itself. And the self alone is a desperate emptiness. In such circumstances, if the poet is wholly the man, no tolerable *form* of life is possible.

Two points to close: *biography* has its roots in βιος and in γραφειν. βιος — life, or *a way of living*; how we go on. γραφειν — to mark or incise, or *to enroll*, to induct or initiate (into) or agree on — a form of life, which is, practically, a community. *Grammar* has a related root.

Lastly, if I may adapt that extraordinary opening sentence from the 1848 *Manifesto*: A spectre is haunting the European Imagination — the spectre of community. Such, I take it, is (part of) the significance of the *MacDiarmid* brackets round the MacDiarmid poems by Christopher Murray Grieve.   **Walter Perrie**

RAYMOND J. ROSS
SPEAKERS' CORNER
EAST PRINCES STREET GARDENS
(In Memoriam Tom Murray)

'There's not a soul in Edinburgh doesn't want salvation.
There's not a soul who wants to go to Hell.'

The voice is slick, American and Mormon.
Dictates to pigeons and to hyacinths,
Reverberates as far as Walter Scott
Who stares unseeing at the past.

Thistles there are drooped and almost dead
With dust from city tours
While down behind the speaker stands,
In shadow of the R.S.A.
Unlooked for and unseen,
A simpler stone which reads:

'To the memory of those who fell in Spain
From the Lothians and from Fife
Erected by the International Brigades.'

And still the speaker rants, oblivious
To ones who scorned salvation of their own
And went at least as far as Hell.
The stone absorbs his words.
Their voices echo back.

JOYCE McMILLAN

THE PREDICAMENT OF THE SCOTTISH WRITER

It is an unoriginal observation, but nevertheless a true one, that the predicament of the Scottish writer is inseparable from the predicament of Scotland itself. In *Scott and Scotland,* Edwin Muir describes the place as '... a hiatus, neither a nation nor a province ...'; in his introduction to the same book, Allan Massie calls it 'a country which has become a sham'. That the political absorption of Scotland into the United Kingdon and the British Empire has been accompanied by a relentless suppression and trivialisation of Scottish literature and Scottish history is beyond doubt; the pressure on every talented and ambitious U.K. citizen to ape as closely as possible the speech, manners and life-style of the English upper middle class has taken its inevitable toll on the richness, the continuity and the self-sufficiency of Scottish culture; and looking back even over my own relatively short life-span, it is clear that there has been a tragic loss, a kind of theft.

I was born into a well-doing, respectable, upwardly-mobile-artisan kind of family, with a pedigree of almost perfect Scottishness for generations back on either side, and brought up in a stoutly Presbyterian village in the west of Scotland; between them my aunts and uncles and grandparents possessed a tremendously rich — if slightly bowdlerised and Lauderised — fund of Scottish language and manners, songs and stories. Yet one of my most powerful memories of childhood is of my mother's concern to train us away from the Scottish speech of the children in the streets round about, and to insist that we speak 'properly' — that is, with Standard English grammer and syntax, English intonation, and only a tasteful smattering of Scottish vocabulary; although, interestingly, there was limits to our admiration for Standard English speech. We drew the line at saying 'little' instead of 'wee', or affecting a really posh accent.

At Primary School, we did history that was shapeless and colourful, and full of Bonny Prince Charlie and Robert the Bruce; we also learned long Scottish poems (with no dates at the bottom) about dead sailors and battles. But in Secondary School, all that vanished in favour of serious, important, shapely history which fitted together like a jigsaw and actually helped me to understand significant modern things like the Labour Party and the Welfare State — and most of that history seemed to have taken place in England. In literature, the same thing happened; the odds and ends of colourful Scottish poetry disappeared when we begun our certificate courses, and we studied real literature that started from Chaucer and finished with Yeats and Eliot; and it was only much later that some little Scottish pieces reappeared — Scott, Burns — neatly slotted into the big English pattern. I don't think I have quite rid myself, yet, of the feeling that Scottish literature and history are somehow for children, whereas the English equivalents are for grown-ups.

Later on, at St. Andrews University, I ran full tilt into what is possibly the most anglicised of all Scottish institutions, and often found myself in classes and coffee-rooms where mine was the only Scottish voice. The Honours English exam. demanded *one* paper out of *nine* on Scottish literature, and that was regarded as something of an imposition by the two-thirds of arts undergraduates who were, in fact, English. But I remember the shock of delight at my first encounter with Henryson and Dunbar, and the sudden realisation that Scots had once been a living, confident, flourishing branch of mediaeval English speech instead of the couthy, whining political plaything into which it had latterly dwindled; and I remember too the moment when I suddenly understood — well into my 20's — that the working-class speech I had been carefully trained away from in my infancy was not just a cheap, scruffy and inaccurate version of modern English but some kind of surviving remnant of real Lowland Scots, the language of

Dunbar and David Lindsay. It is because of this kind of 'Scottish' education that I sit here in Edinburgh today, having lived more than 28 of my 30 years in Scotland, looking Scottish, sounding Scottish, and knowing myself to be Scottish; and yet surrounded by bookshelves full of Shakespeare and Milton, John Donne and Bryon, Jane Austen and Evelyn Waugh, and as ignorant, when it comes to Scottish literature, as the day is long. All I ever had to do, in order to complete my Scottish literary education, was to scribble four short, hasty exam. answers on Dunbar and Hogg, Scott and Burns.

Under this sort of disgraceful circumstance, it's hardly surprising that the Scots tend to see themselves — whenever and wherever a slightly raised level of cultural consciousness breaks out — as an oppressed group. Like women, or blacks, or the economically exploited, Scots came together in organisations — the Scottish National Party itself, groups like the Saltire Society, the persistent Scottish republican tendency within the Labour Movement — to share their grievances and try to win back some control over their political and cultural lives. Many Scottish writers, naturally enough, belong to such groups or at least feel some sense of common cause with them, and they begin, inevitably, to judge themselves by the standards of — through the eyes of — those groups. This is the process Allan Massie describes in his New Edinburgh Review article on James Kennaway, when he says of Scottish writers: 'We are always being tested — perhaps test ourselves — against our Scottishness ... anything not insistently Scottish is ipso facto un-Scottish ...'. The Scottish cultural establishment itself cherishes its hard-won consciousness of the ways in which Scottish culture has been discriminated against, and tends to demand that that consciousness never be let slip; and it is at this point that the artistic rot set in. Because a creative writer cannot play to that the kind of ideological gallery; cannot — if he or she is to progress, break new ground, find new ways of looking at the world — cater for the preconceived opinions and prejudices of any group, however sympathetic and supportive. When I read modern feminist novels, I can often sense, breathing down the writer's neck, a kind of internal group of prefects of cheer-leaders from the women's movement, whose predictable and insistent cries of 'right on' or 'sexist bullshit' can be seen influencing the progress of the novel at every turn. Likewise, a great many Scottish writers seem to be accompanied by a mental band of Scotland supporters, an internal Ally's army who are liable to shout 'English poof', 'snob', 'traitor' or 'we wuz robbed' if any incorrect, English-looking or (god forbid) middle-class sentiments creep into the prose; and this situation is intensified by the fact that the west-of-Scotland working-class has come, in some circles, to be seen as the main repository of genuine Scottish language and culture, so that the self-righteousness of the oppressed working classes and the culturally-robbed Scot comes into play simultaneously.

Of course, writers have as much right as anyone to be feminists, socialists, Scottish Nationalists or Scots and Gaelic language activists. But at the moment when they sit down to write creatively, they must turn themselves from campaigners into explorers, discard their existing mental maps, their fixed ideologies and aspirations, accept themselves as and where they are, and work freely from there. Given the choice, few Scots would have wanted to start from here; I, for instance, might have preferred an education that made a big, seamless, meaningful Scottish pattern of my history and culture, stretching all the way from the broad Scots songs my granny sang to the devolution referendum. But if I've lost a great deal, I've also gained something, in my early training in and continuous access to one of the richest literatures in the world (I mean English Literature); and I am content, in my work as a journalist and critic, to begin from where I am.

There's no doubt, though, that the fear of betraying either their Scottishness, or their working-class origins, or both at once, has a very limiting effect on some Scottish writers. As Massie has observed, it can lead to a kind of infantile quality in style and subject-matter; writers who feel guilt-stricken about the middle-class literary milieu in which they live their adult lives tend to avoid writing about it, and there is a curious tension in Scottish writing between those who actually try to work out of their middle-class experience (Stewart Conn is a good example among playwrights) and are accused of producing material which is not 'really Scottish' — although one might point to a dozen thematic concerns, habits of thought, aspects of atmosphere that mark the thing as anything but English; and those, on the other hand, who worry away obsessively at the 'matter of Clydeside', long after they're capable of producing something more than sentimentalised memories and quasi-realistic chunks of nostalgia about their tenement childhoods. The worst recent example of this kind of writing in the Scottish theatre was undoubtedly Bill Bryden's *Civilians;* but almost every play which deals with working-class life carries some trace of this guilt-ridden, sentimentalising tendency. The temptation to 'edit out' those aspects of personal experience which don't fit in with some preconceived political or cultural ideology is simply fatal to a creative writer; before artists can move anywhere they have to see the truth of their own cultural situation steadily, and see it whole.

The destructive obsession with the need to emphasise and preserve the 'Scottishness' of our writing far beyond what comes naturally and truthfully to writers will persist for as long as Scotland remains in a political limbo; in other words, it will last until Scotland either becomes a full nation-state, or loses its sense of nationhood altogether. That is not to say, however, that no good writing can come out of Scotland until that political millenium arrives, and indeed I think there are several grounds for hope. To begin with, certain gifted individuals have always been able to transcend the cultural limitations with which fate presents them. There are those with a natural self-confidence that enables them to relish and use *all* their cultural experience no matter what their circumstances, and those whose internal compulsion to write truthfully out of their experience is so strong that it completely drowns out the chanting of the mental supporters' club; in Scotland, there are those — still Scots in their way — whose privileged education has spared them the distorting experience of cultural oppression, and those who live out their lives in small rural or working-class communities, never sallying forth to be corrupted by middle-class affluence or Edinburgh ideologies. Such writers will escape the prevailing obsessions of the Scottish literary scene.

Secondly, there are vast cultural movements afoot today which make the internal problems of Scottish literature look relatively insignificant. The Scottish working class may still be the main repository of un-anglicised Scottish language and culture, but over the past 50 years — without much reference to the Scottish literary establishment or, for that matter, to the dominant Oxbridge culture of the British arts and media — their cultural experience, like that of the mass of people everywhere in the West, has become overwhelmingly international. The generation of Scottish playwrights now in their early 40's is remarkable for the fact that they don't care one way or the other about English culture; their ideas on narrative, dramatic structure and style were all formed by American films of the 40's and 50's, their greatest musical influences have been black American jazz and rock and roll. These days, working people in Glasgow are much more concerned about the next episode of *Dallas* than about the survival of Scottish culture in any form, and the persistent preoccupation with Scottish forms of cultural expression and Scottish writing is one factor which, in itself, alienates many Scottish writers from the Scottish working class, who are fully as sophistacted, as up-to-date, as well-travelled and as internationally-connected as any modern Western proletariat. Part of the brilliance of John Byrne's *Slab Boys* trilogy is that is not only sets itself firmly in the west of Scotland in the 50's, and conjures up that society perfectly; it also places it in its context of James

Dean and Radio Luxembourg, and the post-war economic boom that swept the whole of the Western world up in a wave of consumption and prosperity. 'You're nineteen wi' a wardrobe full of clothes — you've got everything to live for ...' as the catch-phrase goes. Unimpeachably Scottish, written in the rhythms and vocabulary of a perfect Paisley demotic, *The Slab Boys* has absolutely nothing to do with the self-conscious preservation of Scots language and culture. It is just a brilliantly theatrical and truthful play about the lives of ordinary Scots in the boom years of the 50's and 60's, and because that truth has far-reaching implications it has proved itself infinitely exportable. A tough, modern, well-made and clear-eyed reflection of Scottish life like *The Slab Boys* will do more, in fact, to affirm and reinforce the vitality of our culture than a thousand carefully-crafted Lallans columns in *The Weekend Scotsman*.

Finally, the part played by women writers in Scottish literary life is increasing, at the moment, by leaps and bounds, and with that development there must come a change in old psychological patterns and tensions. It is a curious thing that women never have been so obsessed with the questions of Scottishness as men; men have always been far more inclined to support the S.N.P., to get hot under the collar about English arrogance, and to feel the whole business of Scotland's colonial status as a personal insult and threat. Why this should be is hard to say. It's tempting to speculate about some kind of Bannockburn complex or Flodden factor, the connection between national military prowess and personal virility. It is also a fact that women in any working-class culture in Britain will tend to speak less broadly than their men, to adapt their language more easily and flexibly towards received vocabulary and pronunciation. Perhaps it has traditionally been more important for men to be seen not to kow-tow to cultural and class domination. But the simplest explanation is probably something to do with football; women far less than men are brought up to attach a profound emotional and personal significance to the hysterical fortunes of the Scottish football team, the very existence of which must be seen as something of a socio-historical anomaly (although I will never forget the look of utter contempt which I once received from one of my uncles when I suggested, in my innocence, that we might do better in the World Cup if we just had a British team), and Paul Pender's fine play *The Game* thoroughly exposes the morass of political, personal and sexual neroses aroused by Scotland's World Cup disaster of 1978.

At any rate, most Scottish women writers seem relatively free from the little-brother complex, the chip on the shoulder, the need to assert and re-assert Scottishness. In writers like Liz Lochhead and Marcella Evaristi, Alma Cullen and Joan Lingard, the Scottishness of theme and manner and often of languages is indisputably there; the need to prove it — the mental team of Scotland supporters distorting and disturbing their personal vision — is not; and their increasing prominence in our literary life can only have a positive and liberating effect.

All writers have predicaments, difficulties, personal limitations of character and experience which cause them problems; but insofar as the Scottish writer has a special dilemma, I think it lies in the particular difficulty, for a culturally colonised people, of developing a strong and uncensorious confidence in the validity of one's own experience — as a man or a women, as a Scot, a European, and what is called 'a citizen of the world'.

Joyce McMillan

ANDREW NOBLE

SCOTT, SCOTT AND SCOTLAND

P.H. Scott's recent little book on Scott* induces a feeling of gloom not so much perhaps because of its particular inadequacies but because it so accurately represents the general level of enthusiastic comment released in Scotland by the 150th anniversary of Scott's death. Our fervid, post-Union compulsion to have a compensatory, fallacious national history — the inevitable consequence of which is the distortion of both literary reputation and form — is unabated. For so brief a book to work, incisive, compressed argument would have been necessary. What we find, in fact, is a text liberally peppered with highly selective quotations from earlier Scott commentators. These quotations are mainly employed to prove two, related theses. First that, contrary to Edwin Muir's belief, Scott was nourished by *all* the varied strata of Scottish society and thought with which he came into contact. Even if this were so, Mr. Scott's studies of Border society and Edinburgh's varied forms of education are far too brief and derivative to carry real conviction. Second, Mr. Scott argues that this cultural sustenance not only produced a major novelist but a heroic figure who incorporated and, indeed, defended the traditional Scottish values and institutions *as far as it was possible* so to do in the early nineteenth century. Scott, it would seem, had the courage of his prudence. Oddly, given the extreme difference between Mr. Scott's political convictions and those of the hyper-anglicised John Buchan, the Scott who emerges from both their work is a highly sentimentalised figure. If such a writer as they describe is to be seen as the centre of his nation it is an extremely soft centre and one which cannot hold against either stringent historical or literary examination.

Neither Mr. Scott's grasp of nineteenth nor twentieth century Scottish literary history inspire much confidence. Given that the principle thrust of his book is against Muir's *Scott and Scotland,* he neither comprehends the extent of Muir's critical genius nor the place of that particular book in the context of *non-academic* Scottish Scott criticism in the Thirties. Scott claims that Muir knew little of Scott. Recent re-publication of Muir's Scottish criticism show this not to be true. More importantly, Scott is quite incapable of perceiving Sir Walter in the comparative context of Muir's critical genius. Muir could place Scott in terms of both the Scottish and English literary traditions. Further, he could judge his stature in relation not only to his English but his European contemporaries such as Stendhal. In comparison Mr. Scott suffers from tunnel vision.

In order to perceive Scott as quintessential to the Scottish literary genius, Mr. Scott defines him in terms of his ability to synthesise fact and imagination. The 'Caledonian antisyzygy' has at least the durability of Nessie. Edwin Muir's case was that Scottish literature since the Reformation has, with few exceptions (incomparably MacDiarmid), dealt not in (Blakean) creative contraries but in a cowardly dualism whereby impoverished fancifulness surrenders to debased realism. He considered Scott to be both victim and agent of this sorry, reduced state. Thus he did not find in Scott that quality of integrated imagination which he discerned in the great English and German ('High') Romantics who were his immediate contemporaries. As Muir noted: 'the romantic movement only commences when deliberate concern with the romantic ends; and its real inspiration falls on Wordsworth, who did not seek romantic themes, and not on Scott, a writer in the classical tradition exploiting legend and history.' Mr. Scott is, of course, not alone in misunderstanding Scott's relationship to Romanticism. Since Lockhart, Scottish *littérateurs* have never been done with narcissistically congratulating themselves on discerning Sir Walter's stability, common sense and realism in comparison to the allegedly self-indulgent illusions of his English contemporaries. What in fact they discern in their mirror is a self-congratulatory bourgeois sentimentality replete with the kinds of personal and political fantasy which, derived from *debased* Romantic sources, has been Scotland's crippling *official* self-consciousness since the late eighteenth century. Tom Nairn's 'The Three Dreams of Scottish Nationalism' remains the most cogent exposé of this state of mind. Romanticism is to be properly understood as an incomplete but profound response to a crisis which was not so much personal as communal wrought, as it was, by the pressure of often brutal utilitarian change. Essentially its aesthetic values were neither diffuse nor escapist. Wordsworth's poetics are exemplary in their desire for the linguistic reclarification of word and thing in the name of social and spiritual truth. Despite his intense private anxieties and frequent uncivil rages about the nature of his times, Scott avoids honest treatment of them. Like Coleridge, Muir believed that much of Scott's enormous commercial success lay in his anodyne power. Muir also believed that in mercenary obeisance to the growing power of proto-Victorian gentility, Scott surrendered up the best, virile elements of both Scottish poetry and the eighteenth century English novel. Nor is this an eccentric judgement. As early as 1831 James Hogg had bitterly complained of the aesthetic and cultural damage which resulted from Scott's bowdlerisation of the Border ballads. Unlike Mr. Scott, he did not see the conjunction of Sandy-Knowe and genteel Edinburgh as fruitful.

Another major error regards Mr. Scott's notion that 'celebrated or notorious' book, *Scott and Scotland,* was an atypical product of the Scott criticism of the writers of the Scottish Renaissance. What made the book unhappily notorious was MacDiarmid's response to Muir's justifiedly pessimistic analysis of the future of Lallans. As Mr. Scott somewhat tortuously admits, MacDiarmid made far harsher judgements about Scott's politics and his relationship to nationalism than Muir ever did. Here Mr. Scott is symptomatic of the most alarming development in Scottish (academic) literary criticism over at least the past decade. There is increasing ignorance (suppression?) of the creative critical dissent present in non-academic Scottish writing in Twenties and Thirties. We frequently seem a fair way down the road to reconnecting with the mendacious, orthodox pieties about Scottish writing promulgated in the eighteenth and nineteenth century 'literary' Edinburgh and by our academics of that time. We have not even assimilated, far less built on, the heroic labours of the pre-War years. In the particular case of Scott, Muir has become an aberrant scapegoat whereas the truth of the matter is that the deepest parallels for his analysis of Scott's failings are to be found in writers of the stature of MacDiarmid, Neil Gunn, the Carswells and Rebecca West. Neil Gunn, for example, in reviewing *Scott and Scotland* wrote:

... Scott himself, in a moment of moving self-realisation, cried out against the historical material he dealt in, calling it 'stuffing my head with the most nonsensical trash.' Scott was so great a genius that what he dealt in must have some reality to the mind of living men. It is not that the history was untrue or was inadequate subject matter for his genius; it was that it no longer enriched or influenced a living national tradition; it had not even the potency of pure legend; it was story-telling or romance set in a void; it was seen backwards as in the round of some time spyglass and had interpretive bearing neither upon a present nor a future. Only some such intuition from Scott's 'secret world' could have drawn from him in his latter years these bitter words.

It is not, of course, entirely true that Scott's fictive Scotland is a partial vacuum with free-floating Gothic and sentimental elements as its sole content. Since Lukács we have all, in one way or another, been persuaded that it conveys an interpretation of history. While, inevitably, Mr. Scott cannot accept this as a portrayal of the evolution of the *British* constitution, he does consider that it is a philosophy of progress derived from the thought of the Scottish Enlightenment. Since Duncan Forbes's 1952 article on Scott this relationship has provided the key-stone for almost every triumphal critical arch erected to the sagacity, even intellectualism, of his fictional vision. This seems to me to represent, at best, a profound naiveté regarding the relationship of fiction to ideas in general and to political and social theory in particular. Facts are the sacred, primary sustenance of fiction. What contemporary life presented Scott with were some very harsh facts which manifested that the melioristic progress initiated by laissez-faire economics had, at the least, some very severe side effects. Hence the astonishing difference in Scott's private political writings and the repressed world of his public fiction. As Thomas Crawford has remarked:

> Scott's difficulties as an artist were due not so much to any defect in the life of the Scottish people — this was an age of industrial expansion and social ferment — as to his Toryism, his pathological fear of radical weavers and contemporary mobs, combined with a refusal to put art first, and a disastrous compromise with the market.

Despite Graham MacMaster's recent interesting attempt in *Scott and Society,* no one has yet explained how this mixture of aesthetic bad faith and fear and anger with what Scott regarded as a disintegrating society was transmitted into unbiased, generous fiction. Should we really trust the tale rather than the teller in this instance? Mr. Scott's case is not strengthened by the fact that he seems to regard the Scottish Enlightenment as he does Scott: that is as an undiluted, ethnic 'good thing'. In fact it was an ambivalent, often cosmopolitan, body of social and economic theory which wrought often fractious and, for a not insignificant minority, impoverishing results because of its innovatory, ratiocinative methods regarding wealth, agriculture, architecture and industry. It was also with Hume and Smith both a hypothesis about and an act of faith in bourgeois man. Arguably this led to the class divisions in Scottish society growing wider rather than the unifying process which they had predicted. Here, of course, we encounter the apparent paradox of not only the Marxist endorsement of Scott but, with regard to its specific approval of Scott's fiction, Mr. Scott's endorsement of Marxism. I would contend with Marxist enthusiasm for Scott shows exactly what is wrong with him as both a national and creative writer. He promoted the entrepreneurial middle-class as subsequent 'socialist realists' did the working class. Both are biased systems of pseudo-scientific economics which lay falsely elitist claim to historical inevitability. In such instances literature becomes the fanciful, mendacious icing on the determinist cake. True imagination is the eternal enemy of ideology. Literature and historicism are not compatible. Scott's work is a formulaic manipulation of language and narrative forms (mainly derived from English comic and German Gothic sources) in the name of theory of 'progress' which was misguided enough in its own time and is now an absurdity among the industrial archaeology of contemporary Scotland.

Thus while celebrating Scott's patriotic stoicism Mr. Scott can never logically explain how nationalism and cosmopolitan, class-defined, economic determinism are to be brought together. Indeed in his penultimate chapter on 'The Consequences of the Union' Mr. Scott gets involved in a series of remarkable convolutions in attempting to define Scott's position as the best form of nationalism available at that point in our history. While Nicholas Phillipson's theory of noisy inaction may be too harsh, Mr. Scott does not convince me that in his nationalistic activities Scott was not involved with peripheral matters of symbol rather than substance. Also the notion of Scott as the healer of the wound between Highland and Lowland Scotland promulgated by Mr. Scott seems to me a manifest absurdity. Scott commercially exploited an appetite for 'primitivism' with the Highlands as its object which existed prior to his work. He was directly responsible for enveloping the whole of Scotland in a false, sentimental 'Celtic' consciousness which has had profoundly bad effects on both sides of the Highland line. Nothing he wrote had any bearing but a dire one on the erosion of Highland life in the nineteenth century at the behest of the new, progressive economics. Mr. Scott's notion of 'Roman' virtue as the essence of Scottish life seems to me equally suspect. If the ascetic core of our character is *pietas, gravitas, industria* etc. we will certainly have to look again at Robert Burns who has generally been accepted as some kind of representative for us. It is hard to see, given that our literature is distinctive by its fusion of eccentric contraries, why such a personality type as defined by Mr. Scott should be the happy or logical result. Heaven knows what MacDiarmid would have made of such a Scottish archetype. As he wrote:

> There are people who imagine that but for the Union with England, Scotland would still be destitute of all the blessings of modern civilisation. They find no difficulty in associating this belief with the idea that Scotsmen are thrifty, hardworking, exceptionally well-educated, law-abiding and home-loving. I am not one of them.

Nor, as Muir brilliantly illustrates in his description of Abbotsford in *Scottish Journal,* was Scott himself a prudent or rational man however well he responded to his self-inflicted financial wounds.

The point, however, is that MacDiarmid and the other writers of the Scottish Reniassance would have seen the cardinal virtues promoted by Mr. Scott as a symptom of the emasculation of the Scottish middle-class which was designed to make them the relatively prospering middle-management of British nineteenth century imperialism. Stoics do *not* make national revolutions. As early as 1832, William Cobbett had seen parallels between Scotland and Imperial Rome in so far as she was like a Roman colony ruled increasingly by an upper and middle class who had assumed anglicised, pro-consular status in order to advance themselves.

Given that nationalism is the true answer to Scotland's sorry plight, there is an element of wish-fulfilment, even fantasy, in looking towards Sir Walter and his works as providing the foundation for such a resurrectionary force. Mr. Scott says we owe Scott a debt of deep gratitude. What he did, in fact, was, for an over-long period, let us off the hook of our national dilemma by suggesting that we could divorce our feelings for Scotland from our practical, often-self-seeking, activities. This led in no inconsiderable degree to the disintegration we now see around us. The SNP is tearing itself apart in class conflict. The heavy industrial base of the nation has almost vanished. Last summer — in the midst of the most insane war as yet wrought by British Imperialism — Mrs Thatcher led the ruddy ranks of the Unionist Party at Perth in singing 'Land of Hope and Glory'. Can we be absolutely sure that Sir Walter's great head would not have provided a stolid but prominent back-cloth to the Leaderene's savage angularity were he still with us? We are not to be saved by Sir Walter by a sense of literary history that accepts Lockhart's *Peter's Letters to his Kinsfolk* as a reliable guide to Scott and early nineteenth century Scotland.

Andrew Noble

Walter Scott and Scotland: P.H. Scott. William Blackwood £5.95.

T. S. LAW

FACT (pairt o a langer work)

The mair ye luk at it, a fact's as bonnie
as neednae boather wi appearances.
An gin it's true the wy that handsome is,
a fact is bonniest whuin daein its dances,
for instance, roond an roon reveesiounism.
A fact is chyngeable as onie wumman
maks maist o laest an best o little better,
yit bydes the same inbye the buskrie.
Whit's aa this nonsense, then, we hear anent
reveesiounism? Whit ist, then, in fact?
As braith can follie braith lik ilka braith
that pecht in tune wi aa tyme ever was,
as tho thae thoosan-thoosan millioun braiths
cuid mak nae differ in millenia;
as ilka braith that puits twoe wurds o this
upon the page can mell wi, modifee
the ootmaist boond o the atmosphere that hains it,
sae ocht avaa that happens efter a fact
as pairt o its bein an continuance,
is naething but reveesiounism. Kick
or no kick onie baa at onie fuitbaa match,
score or score-nane wi't, chip or blooter it,
the result at the whissle will still depend on the wy
yer buits haed fittit or haed fittit-nane.
The fuitbaa commentator daes his speil
on chances taen or missed: it's nocht but yabble,
poleetical yabble at that, an nithin's waur,
for Tapsalteerie tummles-the-wulkies for a leevin.
Was Marx a Marxist, Lenin Leninist?
An whye is Engels no upon Olympus?
Dae deviatiounists aye play the baa?
An dae reveesiounists aye play the man?
'They're aa aff-syde,' say a millioun referees.
Young Waukrif Socialism never bous
an ee afore Doore Daith can pickle saund
upon it for tae steek it wi Auld Tyme.
Aa folk ken weel enyeuch whit follies efter
gettin oot o bed on the wrang syde, never myn
gettin oot o the wrang bed onie syde avaa,
tho we haenae gotten a saw tae sooch at that, yit.
Gif thare was nae reveesiounism cawed
or cawed-nane onie baa aboot a park,
or oniebodie in or oot o bed,
even the status-quo wuid hae tae revise itsel
tae keep fae staunin still an gettin naewhoere:
reveesiounism is the fact o chynge.
The ever-chyngein fact that bydes the same
is the inalienableness o the wurld
fae aa mankyn, no for its exploitatioun
for the yae man or for the yae companie.
Ocht duin bi oniebodie oniegaets
is reveesiounism, whether waantit or no,

whether grantit or no, or whether guid or bad.
It's juist a policie: the real debate
suid be on the parameters atween
the goal-posts, never mynd atween the bed-posts.
Fact is, this gemme is never played in funnie.
Fact is, it's thaem or us for the Cup, ma sonnie.

NAE CAIRRIET STORIE

An Ancient Mariner ahint yer lug,
hear noo that gin we listen-nane tae ken
the stories the auld folk tell o thair young days,
we'll ken oorsels nae mair nor we can ken
oor ain days that we never keek tae see.
We'll be sair puitten-oot tae finnd we cannae
see the days o oor bairns in the licht o kennin thaem
an thur wys o daein onie the better aither.
A generatioun that luks at itsel, as tho
anither haed neever been, bydes aye inbye
its ain nane-siccarness in kennin naither
ocht o pleesure nor ocht o pain fae the past, neever myn
the pleesurin or peetie fae the future:
it brekks the dirlin baun that hauds folk siccar
in the generatiouns wi the millenia,
for aa comes doon tae whit is maklie best,
altho a best as dowlesslie as bad
as nogganheids gan naewhoere but for drams
or pottieheids mak dirlers o thur powes.
Naw, nane can ken whit wy a wurd can gar
a new releegioun soor the saucht o Gode
or the peace o man, onie mair nor the wy a sang
can cairrie a folk's ain eemage o thur kynd aa thru
the wastrie o twoe-three thoosan year an mair.
Whit will the wurd o MacDiarmid dae at the daith
for the lyfe o the kintrie? Here's a storie cairriet
nae furder nor atween twoe freens and you.
In the Saecont Wurld Weire, a wheen o Glesca bairns
were evacuatit tae the kintriesyde
ower Gartmore wy whoere Cunninghame Graham yince badd
afore giein lairdship ower for bunnetskip
at Ardoch. Yae yin o the evacuees,
the wale o aa the squaater o waens, haed taen
guid tent o whit his faither haed said on freedom.
Haein bocht haund-aixes chaep in Woolworth's Stores,
the laud gaed scurrivaigin wi the lave
oot-thru the Gartmore wuids, Ruid-Indian-roch
an yellochin lik Braves. The gemmie taigled
wi him, sair miscaain him for the ploy, sin naething
may be duin in parks or wuids athooten leave
o the gemmie servant or the maister laird.
Lik horsemen, the Greeks haed a wurd, an the wyfies the last,
but nane's lik the wurd the lauddie gied the gemmie:
'The land belangs tae the people, and if ye daenae
lae us alane, we'll cut the heid aff yer bluidie duag!'
Whoe was laird's duag fairgied yon gemmie a shoge.

DIVEENITIE

For thinkin folk, we fairlie scoosh lik peevers
on this wurld made releegious pawldie-beds.
Gin we're aware-nane lyke the thocht o nae-thocht,
we mak diveenitie a name 'Gode-Nameless
      for whit we daenae daur a name tae mean.
Gin we skaith aathing intil daith growne doorer,
we mak diveenitie Gode o Creatioun,
      blythe for the bairnin complements the slauchter.
Gin we ken carkin, wurdless fasherie,
we mak diveenitie the Wurd 'Gode-Praised',
      as tho aathing is sorteit wi a sang.
Gin we are sweerie wi the pagan's Praise,
we mak diveenitie the Gode o Dreidour,
      in case Auld Hangie's hingin-on oor wurds.
Gin we are selfish lyke ill-luve's nane-luvin,
we mak diveenitie the yae Gode-Jealous,
      tae gar him lyke the eemage he haed made.
Gin ilka haet we dae caws ithers doon,
we mak diveenitie the Gode o Maercie,
      lest ithers caw us doon i the bygaun tae.
Gin we are cruel-cauld ayont aa boonds,
we mak diveenitie the Gode-Langtholein,
      sae he'll can ken het-cruel bleezes luve.
Gin we are innocent as slauchtert waens,
we mak diveenitie the Bairn o Gode
      will tak upon Hissel the guilt we're feart o.
Gin we're illtethit, as wi fraucht o pyzon,
we mak diveenitie Gode-Guidliheid
      will waur the smittle cairriet oorsels ben.
Gin we aye cherish weel the fause-puit-on,
we mak diveenitie Gode on the Crosse,
      sae folk ower weel-puit-on are shamed fornent us.
Gin we goam-nane sic freits as luve an licht,
we mak diveenitie Gode-Eemages,
      lest we suid see oorsels whuin we're no keekin.
Gin we gilravage lyke the weires an rammies,
we mak diveenitie the Gode o Saucht
      tae gar the rebels be the sauvages.
Gin we are herried hoose-and-haud oorsels,
we mak diveenitie the Gode o Battles,
      in case some day we mak oor ain excyuisses.
Gin we ken Gode, an say nane ken lik us,
we mak diveenitie the Gode o Faith,
      as tho Nae-faith cuid ken whit ken-nane meant.
Gin we byde bruitlik, sauvage tae the verie tuith,
we mak diveenitie Gode-Fyne-an-Fairlik,
      blythe for tae tell the bairns tae byde mair gentie.
Gin intae hate lik endmaist daith-in-leevin,
we mak diveenitie the Gode o Luve
      for whit thon Auldshanks caas a leevin-daith.
Gin aa men in thur lykeness are deceivers,
gae tell thir things twyce-ower untae Believers.

T.S. Law

COLIN MACKAY

POEM ON A PARABOLA

And I shall close my eyes and see
the city fade away in blue mist,
and feel again the happiness
of strings echoing within me.

I shall return again to the land
from which they took me in the morning,
a captive led without warning,
shackled to a stranger's hand.

Where was the place of my beginning?
the green island of my heart-felt home?
Long have I sought through the ocean's foam
for the hills where the bells are solemnly ringing.

Round and round the madhouse wall
the devils' circle dances,
and I hide alone in my cell
tracing the parabola of memories.

THE CHIMES AT MIDNIGHT

'We have heard the chimes', the fat knight said:
'the midnight chimes have sounded for our sort
who marked the passing day in Cheapside pots
and rode the dark to a moonlit bed.

Remember how we met, Nym, Pistol, and I,
and Hal the boy with the princely heart
who was one of us, or so we thought,
when nights were all a wanton sport
and days lurched drunken by?

Yet there were times when I caught his look
as he thought me drowned in a butt of sack,
and saw the commanding snarl scar his face,
heard the derisive snort behind my back.

I knew, yet wished I did not know,
that my lion cub would grow his claws,
that one day he would become a mouth of laws
and forget the feel of a smoky room
and the sound of a running brook.

And so it was, by power annointed,
he turned away from childish things,
closed his eyes to the fat old lecher
and fed death with the game of kings.

Dead all the boys he took to France,
and Bardolph's hanged and Pistol fled,
and redder red-nosed Nym has bled
behind that last advance.

While I lie here in my bed and weep,
sip thin gruel who once swigged sack,
watch candle shadows on the blinds drawn back,
and hear soldiers marching in the street.'
      . . . . . .
I closed the eyes of the tired old boar
and watched the night out by his side
(my regiment sailed on the morning tide)
and I stared in terror through that door.

For who could have known that it would end so soon,
that with spindly shank and sagging thigh
in a babble of green fields would die
the best loved fool beneath the sky
and minion of the moon?

ON THE DROVE ROAD OVER CALDSTANESLAP

In Spring there was a riding of horsemen over the slap.
Leaden hooves grumbled among the heather roots
and rabbits took their shelter under the stones
as the earth shook.

In Summer a castle was built east of the cairns
and soldiers rode the moorish hilltops.
The cattlemen took the Peebles road
in peace.

In Autumn the last reiver was hanged
near where the road runs now, above the burn.
The spray glistened on his rusting spurs
and the rope creaked above.

In Winter the castle was a ruin of nettles
and fallen stones, and desolation all around.
Horse hooves and cattle hooves and under the grass
and rabbits play on the empty moor.

RAIN AND THE MOON

During the long rains of autumn
the city becomes a crumpled ball of paper
under the weeping moon.

And I sit behind bars in my damp prison
thinking of all the women I have never known,
of all the sweet faces I have never kissed,
of all the soft words that have never been spoken.

Worst of all, I feel my children die within me,
and I think I am a mausoleum of unborn children
where my race, a race of warriors, is dwindling into nothing.

In autumn even the southern hills wear
a grey veil of mourning.
The sun is cold as marble,
and the moon weeps.

ON A MOONLIT NIGHT

The white horseman is riding by;
hoof-falls softly on the earth.
From Caerketton screes his charger springs
down to the bulwarked shore of Leith.

The hills are silent restful things
and the city is a sleeping beast.
Woods lost in fairytale dreams
forget the red roar of the east.

The city crouches, unseen;
its hates have vanished for the night.
The pubs and discos all have closed;
abroad roam cats and orange streetlights.

The current of the horse's hooves
passes beyond mere mortal reach.
Beneath a million sleeping eyes
how still lie the city streets.

Yet dawn will bring it back again,
the trance miscalled reality,
the spied-on cell of waking hours,
the prison of each broken day.

Colin Mackay

ANDREW FOX

COMMANDO

Once he was young and eager
before death surprised him
in a solitude which thrives on pain
        and turned his skin to feathers.

Now he lies prone on the roasting sand
in the open grave of the desert,
compassed by the foothills of a broken helicopter
which form his horizon: his ruined America.

Burnt to a crisp,
                large quills prickle on
the vertebrae of a withered scarecrow whose
flesh has been torn away until
the muscles show. The stuffed head

is preserved by a silver helmet naked
of insignia. On the black wrist
a digital watch
                stolen by a streetwise kid

who ducked into the army to escape
the law; a lean hoodlum wasted,
transformed into his own inept wings
                of feathers, wax and string.

ANGUS D.H. OGILVY

LAMENT

We masquerade a greatness
But we breed mourners
To a loud disconsolate music.
Our wild posturing is granite
From the dark sod moor
Steeped into centuries of self-neglect.
Our minds are layers of shifting patience;
Our bones are filed by wind.

Our grudge held like a stump long dead,
Preserved in simmering peat,
Brags of a failure to succeed.
Old prides survive as drunkards, lords,
As weathered stones.

Our history is a brawl
That hacks its heroes from hard lies,
Makes monumental glories of defeat,
A passion hot with prejudice
And legends of lost men.

From rage of purpose came a condign god
To grapple pleasure with the claw of guilt,
A carrion bird that looms his spectre through sag mists,
A brooding shadow on unconscienced joy.

Beside the warmth of winter fires
We laugh behind our camouflage of selves.
Our ringing songs are echoes from sad hills,
Philosophy that slices to the pith,
Succinct, hereditary, smiling in its face.

Our children curl in sleep.
Outside the welcomed stranger watches ripples
On our dark still waters deep.

A SIMPLE PANEGYRIC

Here's to the men
Who fight the odds
Of compromise with social gods,
Become exceptions to the rule
The genius, artist and the fool.
Insipid is the life and dull
Where all things are predictable.

But blessed be he
Who is not loud
Nor stands out plainly from the crowd,
Accepts his lot nor questions why,
Who lives until he has to die.
Without him sitting on the fence
There'd be no odds to fight against.

CROWS

I wake up to the noise of crows.

You are not here.

I watch them from my window
Cross and cackle over fields,
A stark cacophony!

I think of Hughes' disturbing darkness
Born of crow
As nature forged the weapon of itself.
I think of Van Gogh's last bold blackness
Flapping from the cornfields of his death.
These images indelible,
Indicative of crow.
Once they were birds
And nothing more,
Now black as prejudice
They fill my morning sunlight
Like a war.

You who are gone,
Your side of this large bed
Lies flat and cold
(I do not venture any more
Beyond my borders)
I see you in my certain light,
A metaphor of my invention.
Nor can I undress you of myself,
Begin again,
Like these dark birds you fly confined,
Subjective to a dark defining mind.

GROUSE

Fierce from the heather flair of wings
All hollow vowelled on the pulsive air
The call made rapid
Rattling down the laugh's long throat.

Low level grouse
Blur over contours at the edge of light,
Make sheep to flex their knuckled heads,
Are loud as engines on the honeyed moor.

One . . . Two . . .
The thrash released in duplicate
From coils of root
Turns catapult of bird to double thunder
And the thud of death.
In camouflage an eyeball smokes
Behind the barrels of a butt.

Grouse are the victims of their own unnerve;
Are decoys of themselves to false alarm;
Are seldom seen
Until, like men condemned,
They beat the air
And charge the skies unarmed.   **Angus D.H. Ogilvy**

ANGELA McSEVENEY

SLUM-CHILD

On corporation property,
She revelled in her vandalism
Until authority halted the game
Her rosebud lips opened to reply.
'Fuck off, I'll play here if I like!'

Protesting on principle,
The child was ushered to the gate.
Her face, pressed close, withered a little
As more distrust and scorn
Seeded in the mind behind it.

VISIT TO A MATERNITY WARD

The ward was shaded by half-drawn blinds,
Peaceful with hushed voices. Some women were
Pregnant, swaying like waterfilled balloons.
Others had given birth, their mottled babies
Crumpled in sleep at the ends of the beds.

The one I visited was propped against
Heaped pillows, hands neatly folded. Sometimes
Her belly flickered with life, making her
Floral nightdress flutter. Sharing secrets,
She took my hand and let me feel the kick

'Who are you?' I thought, ill at ease with
Her extra dimension, made nervous by
This person-within-a-person, gorging on love,
Tugging at her attention with reins
I could not reach, and jealously getting
In the way when I leaned across to kiss.

PIT-BING

There arches high the back of the Pit-Bing.
Loose filth hauled deep from the Earth stains the ground
With its shadow, darkness seeping into
The landscape while the soil bleeds rust.

Stunted trees sweat dross, stretching grimy branches
Towards the sky. Sap-starved roots probe the empty
Violation below, while above them dry
Leaves shrivel in the breeze.

With milk-teeth missing, freckled children smile
Like budding flowers and begin to run,
Going to meet the weary miners whose
Feet clatter on streets sided by rows of
Duplicated houses and whose skins tell
Of sweaty labour in cramped darkness.

Behind them the sky brims with blood at
Sunset and the first stars glisten like tears
Above the bucked back of the Pit-Bing.

Angela McSeveney

GEORGE GUNN

THE QUEEN MOTHER DRIVES THROUGH DUNNET 1968

The gouchy bitch now striven & small
Turns the corner from
One decade to the next
The haunting voices she leaves behind

form & duplicate

Early morning howling wind through window
Ghostly shreaded wheat of pain
Small & getting smaller
I, cropped headed, young & daft

Bleary eyed, red lipped & ruddy
Stared crudely, still & bronze
(Her hat, her hat, oh like
A cake universe, so ridiculous

I loved its fabulous presence
& her coat so dead
& strung) the unlovely
Metal whish of car, of power

Her land rover cavalcade because up here
We are slightly rough
This is not quite grouse country
But we are surely slaves, alas

Through the little village glinting
& dumb, slumbering
& sulking under
The Atlantic sky, our flat parallels

Uncaring she rides past, oh wicked mother
I was mucky shoed & far
Too shy to whisper
Bow & arrowed a peeping redskin

Behind an all too Scottish hedge
My arrow was not aimed
At you, lady of another
Time, oh no, but at the Sun

The big egg we hardly saw, for were we not
About to pull down Paris
& lay Chicago low, oh yes
These were itchy times, trembling days

The splattered moments, every year
You poured through here
We did not care
Pale, peat eyed & rigid faced

They watched the ugly thump of monarchy
Parade its ghastly airs
Unusually sucumbed, some laughed
& waved, the sea soft cheeks a mass of doubt

A curious amazement at such a drouth
Of meaning, a congregation
Of point & gape, faces bored
& elemental, eyes blurred & unknowing

          on something strange
              & mistaken

A visitor from a terrible time
Of when she cleared
Hallidale & Strathnaver
For it was she as sure as the Duchess

          of Sutherland

Or the Duke, they plodded down
To coast or Hell
& now she smiling
Waving back, a gesture from a Rolls Royce

          does not right
            this diurnal wrong

Mackay & Gunn & Sutherland, place names
Of a peoples ghost
Hand stubborn Canadian
Australian, Yank, but we forget

As if this is forgiveness built from Time
But in my heart
I do not forget
For 1839 or 1968 a crime is still

          a crime

But with a wave & a smile & a furcoat
& a chauffeured life
Of castle & wealth
The moneyed bric-a-brac of the robbing elite

          she blusters past

I hung my bow & arrow over my shoulder
& walked the starry miles
To Dwarick Head
To listen there to my anger fly

& swoop out, out to the Atlantic
That tearful ocean, I let
My sorrow that was more
Than mine retrace that ancestral route

But she, unknowing, motored on to Mey
& there in the bay, fat
& redundant, anchored
By Scrabsters smiling side, grinned

          The Britannia

George Gunn

KEVIN SUTTON

A CONVERSATION

'There's no need to stare. Did your mother teach you no manners?'

'I am compelled to notice your forked beard, rank and thistley with congealed feathers and fulmar spit. Your prehensile eyebrows with which you gesticulate and test your ideas before speaking. Your tattered bonnet, crested by a display of various feathers. Your slippers fashioned from the necks of gannets. The curious design of your plaid suggesting the flight of geese, and the fulmar bone as clasp. You don't have to fidget and crush crumbs with your thumb. I apologise. I was thinking about the island you spoke of.'

'The twenty seven families? The twenty seven low stone houses, round and roofed with bere thatch bound by ropes of twisted heather and weighted with blue and green stones? The low wooden doors with their wooden locks and keys?'

'Yes, the locks and keys. Why did they have to lock their houses? Surely there were no thieves among the twenty seven families?'

'Habit. You might also ask how the fowlers managed to release their hempen ropes of thirty three fathoms length from the Fiennian ring after a day's fowling on the Hero's Stack.'

'You seem to be drifting away into private and mythical memories. Stay with the familiar. That stone cupboard you call your bed with the famous fulmar feather mattress. The red hearth set in the centre of the black earthen floor.'

'That was where I would lay supine and complain of pleurisy whenever the infallible signs indicated bad weather. On rising each morning the twenty seven families would urinate on the dead ashes of the fire — the men standing and the women squatting — then kick the ashes across the floor and stamp them into the earth. In the spring the floor would be dug up and spread on the fields as manure.'

'What did you eat for breakfast?'

'Puffin steeped in oatmeal. And for supper I had dry, unseasoned gannet cooked in cherry coloured fulmar oil, with a handful of sorrel. Not only did the twenty seven families use fulmar oil to flavour their food, but also as illumination, as a panacea for every sickness, as a solvent, a lubricant, a poultice and as a lustration for their breasts. I dislike the pungent odour but the fulmar is indeed a fabulous bird.'

'Stay with the familiar. The stuffed bird here — did you do this?'

'It helps to pass the long birdless winter, and composing piobaireachds with the Jew's Harp.'

'Can you tell me any more about fowling then?'

'I was never one for fowling, you understand. I couldn't stand the heights. The terrible cliffs and perilous crags, you know. I can tell you about puffins though because I went with the women (wonderful straight-backed women) to the scree tumbling toward the sea, where the puffins had usurped the rabbit burrows. These jocular and inebrious birds with puffed up breasts and haughty beaks were regarded as beneath the dignity of the cragsmen.'

'Yes?'

'There were two ways to catch puffins. The first involved the mischievous island mongrels being encouraged to enter a burrow, whereupon the startled puffin would seize hold of the hair on the dog's back believing it was doing a sensible thing. The dog continued on its way, happy with its work gathering appendages through several sets of burrows, until it emerged bristling with irate puffins.'

'The other way?'

'We would set our snares over a concentrated area of ground, catch one puffin and tether it in the middle of the area. We would then retire a little distance and I would listen to the women comparing puffin recipes and the nocturnal performances of their weary cragsmen. I had a few special recipes myself, you know. Anyway, the outraged pandemonium of this one trapped bird brought dozens of other curious cousins to the scene, who promptly found themselves in the same position. Very simple actually.'

'Very. You didn't participate in ... nocturnal performances yourself then?'

'I knew you would be asking that. Well I did, yes I did. Every sabbath. The twenty seven families were not assiduous sabbatarians, you know, nothing solemn. The Lord's Prayer, the Creed, the Ten Commandments. That was all. Every sabbath I would tether my cow to the post in the Idiot's Well and call on the widow of number five.'

'The Idiot's Well?'

'Why must you be changing the subject all the time? Of unknown benediction. Had a cure for every form of idiocy. The power of fascinations. The malignity of elves. St. Vitus' Dance. A cure against left-handedness as well. A great, great, endlessly great grandfather of mine first went to the island to seek a cure. He was said to be under the illusion that St. Bran was being torn between two giant rams on North Ronaldsay. After a week with the well he changed his saint to St. Conan, his great rams to ice-maidens and his isle to Spitzbergen, off Lochlann's northern shores, you know. And then the well turned brackish, and within a month had completely dried up, leaving my endlessly great grandfather with his evolving illusions in motion. He stole a cassock from an itinerant priest and became a keen man for guilling the guillemots. Pulling the cassock on and tying a rope of thirty three fathoms around his chest he stepped blithely over massive cliffs and hung there through the night. Guillemots mistook him for a guano covered rock and came to roost on his shoulders. He kept tucking them under his belt until dawn found him all girdled with guillemots.'

'But so far you haven't told me much about yourself. You say that you didn't fall for fowling, so to speak?'

'I couldn't. Call it cowardice, call it weakness, call it what you will. Dangling and gyrating like a marionette beneath the angry glower of a gannet's eye? Being spat in the eye with half a pint of fulmar oil? No, no. Mind you I did like listening to their reports of second sight as they hung there amidst those galaxies of circling birds.'

'Shall we start at the beginning? When were you born, seems a good place.'

'I was born on a Friday, an unlucky day, you know, the same day that Adam and Eve bit the apple. The twenty seven families recalled the unexplained appearance of the cuckoo that year, but nothing ostensibly unusual had occurred to warrant the arrival of this evil harbinger. Only I was born at noon, under a hot midsummer sun. Or perhaps it was a humid, almost saturated sabbath evening, with a clarified buttery moon in the east and fiddle-headed ferns plucking piobaireachds while the midden heaps squinted and clamoured at the back of the twenty seven houses. Who knows? Who cares? I grew into a mildly handsome youth and poor cragsman. I waxed into a lusty batchelor and finally the same musical older man you see before you.'

'Please go on.'

'I shall start at the beginning then. It was a frosty morning in the spring. Iceberg white clouds still calving and drifting south down an otherwise arctic blue sky. I had been fishing in the creek and was walking back to my house, the littlest twenty eighth. I had a bag of parboiled limpets in one hand and a string of herring in the other. The women were working the querns in couples before the twenty seven houses, naked from the waist up. Straight backs, and breasts — big and little, old and young — swinging to a steady rhythm. I, the failed fowler, the cracked cragsman, suddenly had an overwhelming desire to put a feather in my cap.'

'So to speak.'

'The idea must have been waiting to be thought, it was so clear and formulated. I said I had seen a Greek Auk, the grandest and most stately bird, the prince and philosopher of the fowl kingdom. It is known how the Great Auk lives most of its life at the bottom of the sea, because it is such an awkward flyer and an awkward walker but is a tolerable swimmer. It is presumed that it only steps onto the land to lay its solitary egg. So I chose a beautiful blue stone from the roof of my house, shaped like an egg, and I told twenty seven families that it was St. Moluag's famous blue stone, given to me by a Great Auk. I told them that the saint said it was wrong for them to eat the flesh of fowls, calling it melancholy meat and the fulmar a stinking gull. They were not to eat eggs either as they were bad for the blood, but they must eat fish instead. This dumbfounded the cragsmen who could only complain that their skin erupted whenever they ate fish.'

'Interesting.'

'Then I told the women that St. Brigit had given me a hymn to teach them. A hymn that would save all their bairns from wasting away with the terrible eight day sickness. You know about the eight day sickness I presume?'

'Never mind. Keep going.'

'I met with more compliance from the women. I would accost them singularly and take them somewhere quiet where I would sing softly and oh, so sweetly the hymn of St. Brigit, which explained the cause of the sickness as lying within their very wombs.'

'Don't tell me. It was those wonderful straight backs.'

'I worked my way over eighteen of the twenty seven straight-backed wives, before lifting the skirts of the nineteenth heroically virtuous wife, who held up St. Brigit's hymn for the felicitous nonsense it was. Her cragsman, built like a boat, rowed up and down the front of the house, white faced and exceeding wroth as he called for the other twenty six families. He brought me alongside, and his wife writhing and bridling as though she were being tickled.

'I remember that he discharged a volley of words into the ear of a tunnel spider's nest he had noticed in the wall of his house. You know the stuff. Corruption. Sweetness of true liberty. Deceit and dissimulation, and of course the Brindled One. They were unanimous (the men, that is) in sending me here, to the Inaccessable Stack, and this house of Stallir, the eater of rocks.'

'Pardon?'

'Stallir, that holy hermit, lived his three score years and ten by biting the solid rock with his teeth and scraping the meagre dust together in an earthenware bowl made a thin gruel with the addition of his salty tears.'

'I see. The twenty seven families? The island? Where are they now?'

'The following summer all the birds suddenly arose and left the island, disappearing into the west. Everywhere was uncannily still. As I gazed toward the island it struck me as a very flimsy and insecure affair, no more than a tent upon a vast ocean. Then, as I gazed the island began to tremble and shake and before my bewildered eyes it collapsed into the sea with an elemental boom. Twenty seven families and all. But where are you going? Did your mother teach you no manners? You've not told me anything about yourself. Who are you? Come back here.

Kevin Sutton

ALAN BRUFORD

SCHOOL OF SCOTTISH STUDIES? WHAT'S THAT?

The name 'School of Scottish Studies' suggests a national institution. In practice it is the nearest thing that exists to a national archive of Scottish traditions; many of us who work there feel this should be recognised by a change in status. But I have just had a visitor from Dundee who had great difficulty in finding what or where the school was. It is a department of Edinburgh University, housed on the surviving West side of George Square in the shadow of the new University Library. That too may give a wrong impression. When the folk magazine *Broadsheet* announced our current appeal for funds, one disgruntled reader wrote in to say that *he* was not going to support 'this Ph.D. factory with its cluster of cosy academics inventing work to justify fat salaries and comfortable conditions.' Most readers of *Broadsheet* know better — the first letter was so crushing that the editor closed the correspondence forthwith, and is now being besieged by readers who want to have just one more kick — as might most readers of *Chapman:* in fact, some of the School's staff have given up fatter salaries, or the chance of them, for a job they believe in. All the same, let me try to answer that accusation and it may help to show what the School is.

Inventing work is the last thing we need to do. People whose memories are worth recording die in Scotland every day, and our dozen part-time fieldworkers have not had time to visit one in a hundred of them. What an archaeologist would call 'rescue digs' could easily take up all our time. Already postgraduates have taken over much of the fieldwork from the permanent staff: in time we hope local history groups and community education projects, with encouragement and advice from us, may be able to take over in their own disticts. Even then a good deal is bound to be missed.

What we are recording may take the form of photographs, films, videotapes, or at a pinch — for shy people or brief encounters — notes written up from memory, but normally we depend on sound recordings. The School settled down quite soon after its foundation in 1951 — when it was intended to be a quite different sort of interdisciplinary institute of advanced studies — to be a place where all the researchers, whether they studied pibroch or place-names, did fieldwork with a tape-recorder. The result is an archive of recordings made throughout Scotland — most of them, so far, in the North, especially Gaelic-speaking areas, but that has been a matter of time and urgency, — and, especially if equipped to deal with larger numbers of visitors and correspondents, we should be considered a national institution. (The only comparable sound archive in Britain is in the Welsh Folk Museum: England has nothing like it. The Museum, like most 'folk life' or 'regional studies' institutes in Europe and the Third World, is a government department run by civil servants — not always a good thing, but it means national status and less risk of cuts.)

So what are these recordings about? 'Folklore' sounds airy-fairy, 'ethnology' rather clinical; 'folk life' is better, but tends to include material objects, which we leave to the museums — we collect traditions. The first fieldworkers tended to ask 'Do you know any old songs or stories?' (with remarkably good results often enough) but now we know that 'What did you have for dinner when you were a child?' gets an answer far more often, and may lead on to all sorts of details of social life and in the end to beliefs and stories and music. So much has changed everywhere since 1914 that anything an old person remembers, or a younger person remembers Granny telling them, can be of value to students of what is now called 'oral history', and maybe that is the best blanket term for what we collect — tough it has to be stretched a bit to cover fiddle music. It is about the past, certainly, but it involves living people's memories of what they have experienced themselves, or what their family went through: it adds a personal dimension to the official record, and may reveal details and attitudes that social historians have missed.

No need to invent work at the next stage either: topics for research not only in history, but in literature, music, geography, linguistics, sociology, even economics or psychology pop up in the results of every field trip, and you cannot help following up the best of them. For instance nobody seems to have realised how many people, including most good storytellers, remember a narrative in the form of a series of pictures: the idea emerged in conversation with an old storyteller in Uist, and the research it has led to may reveal something new about the human mind everywhere. If the really cosy (not to say hidebound) academics scoff at our undisciplined, un-pigeonhole-able activities, maybe they are jealous. There were two other small but lively departments teaching folk-life studies in British universities. Unluckily for them, they were in schools of English, and offered a multitude of brand-new thesis subjects for postgraduates as an alternative to yet another study of Spencer's use of allegory, or alliteration in *Pearl*. One is about to close, the other has already ceased full-time teaching, quietly strangled by their colleagues in the name of economy.

We are not so cosy, then, nor were we ever typically academic: the doors of this ivory tower are always letting people out or in. To use a personal testimony, such as we constantly collect, I knew that the School was the one university department where I really wanted to work after a single visit and a meeting with the late Calum I. Maclean (brother of Sorley MacLean and no respecter of academics himself, but the sort of man any housewife, tinker or skipper would be glad to talk to). You could get to know Scotland there: you could help to keep alive what might have been lost (one of my obsessions); but most of all you could combine the sort of scholarship I had been trained for with going out and meeting ordinary, and extraordinary, people. Anthropologists study people, but mostly overseas; sociologists use people nearer home, but to answer their questions; we avoid questionaires, and whatever we may set out to find, when we find good 'informants', who love their own community and its roots, we give them their heads and let them tell us whatever they think is worth telling.

Of course we may have to select, a song you've never heard, needs to be recorded more than one the singer learned off the TV last weekend. But in general people who love their own culture and community are the best judges of what should be kept from it. Several generations of them, better still: the filter of oral transmission is more reliable and more ruthless than any panel of judges. A song may get into the Top Twenty today because of an attractive singer, a cunning agent or a catchy arrangement, but if it is still being sung at the kitchen sink a hundred years later it must have qualities of its own in words or tune. And though we no longer concentrate only on songs and stories, we are still finding ones that are new to us. Scotland's famous respect for education too often bred contempt for what was not in print (or in English!) and now mass culture threatens to swamp what local lore is left. But it can still be found in close-knit communities, or where ability to read English never mattered much: in islands, or where Gaelic or very broad Scots are spoken, or above all among the travelling people, the tinkers who made use of all that the more sophisticated threw away. We may collect no more hour-long Gaelic hero tales now, but a handful of travellers are still remembering unrecorded long Scots wonder-tales — fairy-tales if you like — of a kind everyone thought lost over a century ago. And there remain fields — urban legends and jokes, playground games — where we have hardly scratched the surface yet.

We don't just sit on what we collect, or put it away for private research. Fireside ceilidhing may never come back, but we hope the traditions we have preserved can be given back to the people and handed on in some form. Already the seeds gathered in this dry autumn of the printed word are being sown again in the spring of broadcasting

— so far mostly on local radio, Gaelic and folksong programmes. A steady trickle reaches the public also through Scottish Tradition records and cassettes, our journals *Tocher* and *Scottish Studies* and other publications. And we try to answer reasonable enquiries, and index our recordings fully to make them more accessible to researchers. We can not hand out songs, apart from those we publish, free to anyone who wants them to sing for profit (this may be what annoyed *Broadsheet's* correspondent): our informants are not only custodians of a tradition but human beings who would like their contribution acknowledged if not paid for, and may not want to hear some guitar-thumper murder what their mothers sang.

'Ph.D. factory' — we turn out a few, rather more M. Litts. Our postgraduates have included some from new national folk life institutions in developing countries: we haven't been able to offer any of them jobs here, though when we first started teaching we congratulated ourselves that we could train our own successors (none of our present research staff had much training for the work they are doing). Since 1971 we have started teaching two undergraduate courses as well as a good number of postgraduates; since 1971 we have trebled our publication output with *Tocher* and the records as well as *Scottish Studies*. Since 1971, also, the number of our staff has not increased at all, and is now rapidly falling because University policy (of necessity) is not to replace anyone who retires or resigns except from the most vital teaching posts. So, far from inventing work to justify fat salaries, we are underpaid, understaffed and snowed under with work which we, and most of our pupils, readers, listeners, enquirers, helpers and informants believe is vital to the continuation of an important part of Scotland's national and regional culture. This is why we have to appeal for money to pay for more workers, more equipment and expenses for fieldwork. If you can help at all, please write to: School of Scottish Studies Appeal, 27 George Square, Edinburgh EH8 9LD, Scotland.

Alan Bruford

(This article expresses the personal opinions of the author, not the official policy of the School of Scottish Studies or the University of Edinburgh.)

EDITORIAL NOTE: 'Sireadh bradain sicir' by Aonghas MacNeacail is a poem in ten sections which resulted from an invitation by the artist Simon Fraser to furnish a text in Gaelic for a series of etchings he has done, in which various Norse and Gaelic themes are interwoven.

I should like to apologise, particularly to William Neill and Douglas Gifford, for the misprints which appeared in the last number. These crept in after the final proof-reading, and illustrate the problems which may be experienced by the human race in coming to grips with new technology.

T.S. LAW

THE NATIONAL COMMUNITY

The history of the national movement in Scotland is a record of splinter and fracture, so much so that it seems an extension of the Scottish character. It is time now and past the time to put an end to our divisiveness and thus prevent the continuation of alien rule. As far as the individuals and their pet phobias are concerned, they must decide now that national independence is of far more importance than doing-down a personal enemy. We have little time available, for we have among us a strong and unscrupulous fifth column: if we do not move quickly, we shall have to sustain those people to our detriment until they educate themselves or have education thrust upon them from whatever source, for they are very ignorant. Even now some of them must see themselves as we are used to seeing ourselves, that is, as guinea pigs for future legislation covering the whole island. The lesson they have to take from that is this one, once they begin to learn:

Yince, feelin waabit, dowie and duin-doon,
we thocht we were capootert.
Noo, better educatit for our pains,
we ken we are computert.

There are reasons, and they are always good reasons, why such a movement as ours should throw-off dissidents. It is time now to be unreasonable. That dissidents should create new parties, groups, cliques etc. is not surprising, because dissension itself is the result of excess mental and/or physical energy. It is time to retain such energy in the central powerhouse: if we are to waste power, it must be used to waste the enemy.

Those of us who are members of fringe groups, or groups allied to the central idea of independence, should do all we can to sustain the national movement. We should be seen to be doing so, and we should make clear to friend and enemy alike just why we act as we do. Attitudinising is to poseurs as posturing is to stookies.

It is necessary to know the enemy, for he will not always disclose himself to us. On the other hand, there is no need to know our friends for they will always make themselves known. The enemy is the Unionist first and foremost: an Imperialist in England and a quisling in Scotland. Whether the ultimate Tory traitor, the Liberal falseface, the Labour turncoat home ruler or the Social Democrat faker, they are pretentious without presence. All of them are one and the same enemy, each and everyone a denier of independence. Every word they speak is dummy-articulation spoken to reiterate that denial; everything they do is done as by puppet-manipulation to make that denial as sancrosanct as the Noh gestures of Japanese plays. They have to say and do thus because the denial must be made. Yet, as we know, truth needs no propagandising, while denial is needed wherever traitors gather en masse for mischief or coorie singly in their nyeuks for very shamefulness.

They are outwith the National Community. They do not belong. They are of consequence to it only in their enmity, a pack of messans savaging us. They are to be made ineffective, held at arms' length, they are to be circumvented. They should never be trusted, never given positions of trust. They should not be allowed to influence independence policy on any ground whatsoever, not by their counselling caution, not by their tears (crocodile), not by their supplications. And certainly never by their threatening us with fire, water, rope, knife, gun, bomb, poison, prison, nor by disappearances as in the latest viciousness of fascist countries. (Have you heard the one about the Argentinean who said of his country: 'I wouldn't be found dead here with Galtieri'?). Faced with these things, we must remember:-

> They birled the bannock on Wallace,
> an thocht it wuid dae thur turn,
> but the son o the man that killt him
> was birled at the Bannock Burn.

Nor should our home-grown enemies be placated or given sustenance either by word or deed. We should not compromise with them because they have never compromised with us. And when they come into the National Community (as they will do when we are spreading the butter on the bread), they must neither except nor be given anything but the pleasures or knowing that they are beginning to do what they should have been doing all along. They will have learned by then that if they are to be exonerated for their past conduct, it will be by their children, for Scotland's children must become our new implacable people, the sort who just will not bury their heads in the sand in trying to ignore the howling of the fascists such as the National Front and the yowling of the miserable Imperialists such as those of that infamous Scotland-is-English campaign some years ago.

> It is poetic justice the word 'traitor'
> rhymes alter ego with 'collaborator'.

Trying to psych a Scots international footballer, an opposing English player said, 'You Scotch are just a shower of bloody animals.' The Scots player looked at him: 'Ay, and don't you bloody-well forget it.' Generally, we are too finely-tuned as people or poets of our people to resent insult when met with a company we had thought accommodating. It is perfectly all right for the foreigners to insult us as long as we remain ladylike or gentlemanly enough not to retaliate and thus invoke their rage.

> Whan fremmit folk we met
> an weel-met we wuid be,
> we dae oor wee bit dance
> afore that companie.

If all makars were as mealy-mouthed as that, you would never read an article like this which infers that we behave uselessly in being outgoing to welcome enemies who know as well as we do what they have done — they know they have done us. Put the hames on them at all times. Haul them up on their haunches. Once, there was an Englishman who said, 'Ah, but you know, we are the Masters.' That is something never to be forgotten. Nor should we ever forget to let those kind of people and their quislings know that we remember them both for it. On the inside panel of my study door, pinned beneath a map of Scotland, is a newspaper cutting printed just before the fraudulent 40% Referendum: it bears the legend 'Forty-three well known Scots from the world of entertainment, sport, and the arts declared themselves against the Scottish Assembly yesterday'. The names are listed for our execration or kudos as the humph comes up the back, though I fail to discover the Arts among them. The National Community should always keep the enemy in view like that, and retain for its own use against him something like the following.

BLACK BLESSIN

> It's no I naither lyke the man
> nor his evil, sleekit ee,
> but whan he's hoastin, aye I sooch,
> 'Dee, you bastart, dee.'

> An tho he'll never get tae Heeven,
> and Hell'll no admit him,
> aye I sooch whan I hoast masel,
> 'Smit the bastart, smit him.'

However, among our friends, among our own kind, among those who are with us, we should be tolerant and helpful, generous of our time and talent. We should be kindly, we should warn with forbearance and gentleness, and we should not say anything to their public discomfort and to the joy of the Imperialist enemy. Already we have seen such manifestations of national awareness. We have seen the manner change and the eyes light-up at the sight of a sign or the sound of a word that puts us inwith the commonality of our kind of National Community.

So that we recognise ourselves for what we are, so that we understand why we are, we should begin to underline attitudes. Everything that is peculiarly Scots must be made or remade our own without equivocation. We should spell out quite legibly those things that are ours and about which we just will not tolerate alienation: our land, our seas, our institutions, our languages, our history and our education. Above all, our education, for with it, everything else will follow. There is to be no compromise. We have to make a series of intellectual Reddments to counterbalance the physical Clearances. And in the end, if we do not know it will mean great hardship, then the only place we shall have in the independence movement will be that of sustaining better and hardier people who will thole it for us. Our role will be none-the-less valuable. In that time, how can there be a place for quislings?

RENEWAL

Tae destroy us as Scots,
hoo lang has it taen?
As lang as it taks
tae mak Scotsmen again.

Och, it's angersome butt,
an gy fashioulyke ben
sic a weed in the hert
maks cankerous men.

Til the waather weare roon
we maun thole the auld pain
as the weerd o the year
drees the wuin an the rain.

Whitlikken a kinna
thing's that for tae hain?
Tae say it's tae ken it.
An that's whit we're sayin.

Syne, mair lyker oorsels,
an that wy remain
nae better nor ithers,
but Scotsmen again.

Nothing is to be left to the enemy at home, neither song nor poem, nor legend, nor colour in dress or banner. They have forfeited song and poem, sometimes even giving them to England, though one of them by Thomas Campbell in his 'Ye Mariners of England' has ambiguous lines with which I have no quarrel:

'The meteor flag of England
Shall yet terrific burn.'

The common minstrels of Dunbar's Edinburgh had no tune but 'Nou the day dawis' and 'Into June'. Our enemies at home have no tunes, no songs of their own, certainly not 'Nou the day dawis' for that is the air used for 'Scots Wha Hae', a song they abominate. As they have nothing to sing to themselves, they have nothing to sing to us; and they have nothing to say because they are deracinated. As they have nothing to say of themselves, they give shameful lickspittle lip-service to their Masters. Yet while it's anathema for them to mention Scotland, they cannot now bring themselves to slaver at the mouth over the word 'England' as they used to do. That name remains the talisman of their Master. They are fish people who mant in free air. Their stories and legends have all to do with the betrayal of their fellow-Scots by their ancient and notorious kin: where the guilt of their ancestors is glaring and their acquiescence to it a secret shame, they glamourise the deceit and lie brazenly and treacherously to the school-children. They delight in concealing opinions such as this kind of writing, and concomitantly, love to prevaricate, even to the extent of self-deception, hoping that everyone else may be so deceived. They have usurped our delight in colour, and made the tartan another name for Balmorality: in their hands even a bit of cloth is corrupted to the abnormality of disgraceful burlesque. Where it is used on stage or screen, it is spat upon even while money is made of that salivation, as witness the 'entertainers' among the No-people. Much the same thing is done to the langauges in our mouths by entrepreneurial panderers of innocuousness in all its forms from that same Balmorality to mind-bending and brain-baffling. But they do not remember that the Scots tongue that can so readily praise the true Scottish place is equally adept in flyting at the false Scots face. And they have forgotten that their fellow-Scots can smell-out treachery better than any African witch-doctor.

But we will make the tartan our own again, we will make sure the sky-blue and cloud-white of the Saltire is ours to wear. And we will be sure that when we wear the red and gold of the rampant lion, we wear what was always ours to hold and withhold. And when those things are done with careful knowledge and certain deliberation, we shall have put paid to sham and shame and shall have come into our own and become whole. We shall have been to Schiehallion, the magic mountain of the Caledonians and shall have taken the cure. We shall have established an idealised and unvarying norm for Scotland. It will be good. It will be ours. It will be Scotland made.

THE FREE NATIOUN

Preeve you tae me thare's natiounhood,
and I sall preeve thare's nane;
an that's as gyte as your belief
that needs nae pruif tae ken.
And I can preeve ayont belief,
ayont corollarie,
no dae the-noo means never dae
an Scotland never free.

Preeve you tae me thare's natiouns nane,
and I sall preeve thare's yin,
for that belief bydes ben belief
lik marra ben the baen.
And I can preeve ayont belief,
ayont corollarie,
gif we dae noo an dae nae mair,
then Scotland will be free.

Sae let the unthinkable be thocht
lik a fire-flaucht thru the haerns,
that the unsayable be said
lik thunder tae the bairns;

An let the unwurkable be wrocht
lik a spaein ben the speirin,
that the unmakkable be made
lik het and hammered airn;

an let the unseeable be seen
lik the endmaist revelatioun,
then the undaeable will be duin
an Scotland made the natioun.

T.S. Law

STEWART McGAVIN

from G de Nerval (Vers dorés).

dae we fowk think alane, here
whaur speerit bides aa owre?
we may no see its lowe, but,
jist wha micht share our pouer?

ilk beast has a mynd quick as our ane
ilk flouer a soul apen tae see.
in hard airn lies uncanny luve
aa feelan, warkan on ye.

dree the speiran o the blin waa
the stieran stuff itsel can dae,
almichty's sake pit't tae nae ill yaise

aft in a drumly body bides a Guid
an unborn ee ablow its ain ee string
pure speerit growes inby a chuckie stane.

the first combine

I hae jist seen
the first combine
o the hairst, an
thocht o gowks
i the spring, but
a combine can
be unco bonnie
i the gloaman
or nearer daurk
wi a ring o gowd an
loom o gowdan stour.
flauchtran blades
an the hale muives
wi a bumman soun fae
nocht intil nicht.

doup

ettlan efter a Scots word
for chair, the University kin'
i the dictionar.
a fand doup.
whiles,
it micht dae fine.

selkie

I saw yer whiskert frien
the day, closer in this time
whaur the boat lies.
maistly heid on, wi's
whiskers out.
we spak.
an whiles he turnt
his profile, wi's
heid richt out.

I think

we pairted friens.

aye time for clash
(adapted from Robert Frost)

whan a frien pits his heid roun the door
ettlin for a crack nae dout,
I dinna sit an glower aroun
at aa the darg I hinna dune
an skreich out frae ma sait 'whit is't?'
na, na there's aye time for clash.
I sneck aff ma spectrometer, canny like
it cost a wheen bawbees, an
dauner outby jist
for a frienly veesit.

I dinna unnerstaun

do I no wark eneuch
am I no wyse eneuch
or is't owre kittle
or mebbe
daes the teacher no
unnerstaun himsel
or daes he fankle it
or mebbe
daes the scriever jist
ettle tae shaw
hou gleg he is
or mebbe
is the hale thing sae
tedisome ye maun be
glaikit tae thole it
or mebbe
jist mebbe daes the
hale jing bang no mak
ony sense onywey.

575/2

they'd no hae pizzent
Socrates the day, jist hae
smoorit him in bumf

Stewart McGavin

CHRISTOPHER WHYTE

SLEEPING HERMAPHRODITE
(for Carlos Timon Moliner)

Rome, Galleria Borghese

It is asleep and carefully conceals
with slightly raised shoulders and an animal pressure
of rapt trunk into the receptive landscape
of the couch his and her rich ambiguity.
In wild finesse the head withholds itself
from statement of male or female, or of age:
no stern down pushes round these rosy, curved cheeks.
A light smile, overflow from who knows what
ambivalent dream, dampens for a moment its lips.
A trammelled youth is here,
bloom open now so far and never further,
no wisdom gained by years spent in the chase
of woodland loves or nymphs or boys or fawns.
Her robe's light cadence, there, above the thigh
half-shields his mystery, the dimpling of two breasts,
wet, enticing hunger. Around an encrusted whorl,
a spring long dry, stretches a land of light
smooth skin: dips and depressions the sun has caressed,
breathing off the spangled humour of swim or sweat
from slopes that lift a little as she breathes.
Now branches like thin hands join overhead.
A dim forest. A track leads on, and down
to sacred groves no knowledge has profaned,
or comprehension uttered. From fountains
Earth's sweet liquors endlessly distil,
bright gums, draughts of a sweetness, and a presence
in that floreal cavity dimly discerned.
Astounding plenitude, that doesn't forbid
the upspring of Another: waxen taper,
discoursing summit, reaching, tenuous, there.
        The torso's dormient tranquillity
belies such conflicts, this duality
the artist's pious disposing arm has fashioned
in rest. Pass on, spectator, pass the secret
to whiteness entrusted, time has not disclosed.

        Aristophanes then spoke the truth
when, joking that we'd all be bas-reliefs,
half-nosed, one-cheeked, if piety was still
neglected, he told of the world's first populace.
        There were three races:
Man, and Woman, and Hermaphrodite.
And men then were like spheres, for faster movement,
their limbs distributed with fairness round
each hemisphere, and fertilized themselves.
The first unpiety disjoined each globe,
the face was twisted round, the parts of generation
(now that seeding was topographically impossible,
and the unfruitfulness of embraces threatened
to carry retribution too far) jerked
to the front where, pensive, they still beckon.

Man came to man, woman to woman, great
lovers these, desirers, piners who, fulfilled,
can scarcely recognise their longing's answering act.
And male came to female,
bridging the gap,
smithies of difference,
forging unlikeness to a greater whole,
opening that eternal conflict of one flesh or two,
escaping into another body, ever caught up
in desire, ever an offered, kinetic outward
move to the other, ever reknowing
the separation that annuls, quiets
but cannot deny their unity. Wise Aristophanes.

And that the race might be prolonged they planted
the seed one in another, tangled in embracements.

Can this chill marble then give birth?
O waiting womb . . .
The little god had died. Its sucking lips,
paper-dry, crisp to kindle in the sun,
stopped seeking. With our fingers we had scratched
channels in the sand, hoping to squeeze out
the few last drops of moisture.
Do not die, demigod.
Our precious bundle, temple-thievery,
revolting little abnormality.
And then the hopeless homicide in the dry crater,
where even our sweat was only a moment upon us;
from the revenge on such impiety,
o demigod, save poor Encolpius.

He lived through symbols. In his world
not book, or stone, or desk, or dish
could persist unredeemed, but drew
its being only in interpretation.
These dry bits and fragments,
all that is not other,
this world of its,
would have destroyed him.
To him objects emerged fully-clothed,
the stamen, or the pistil, from the cup,
the space around them crammed
with their relation. Emptiness so burgeoning
he reeled beneath the weight
of such connectedness.
Bed is not to him bed, but house, home, womb,
the body, mother, woman's clothing welcome.
(And so, saying 'evening', a man says much.)
Our world to him is not
enough interpreted.

Sing then the waiting, bearded brides of Argos,
intent upon their husbands' coming, or
he who in Cos stood by the door on guard,
a woman for his woman, prepared

for the mute exchange of token and essence,
the great put-into-play, the mingling
from which neither could ever emerge the same;
bewail our kindred led down to the sea,
destroyed in water that their too unclear
divisioning might not pollute the land
of one stuck fast in certainty. Libussa,
Myros, and children exposed upon the hill
in sacrifice to the great unnamed God.

Stay in my mind, o rich duality:
mental self-fertilizer, all the wealth
of male and female combined in one,
contactive and productive, spilling out
juices that will dissolve and separate
reality, will penetrate
the outermost appearances of things
to bring home rich confusedness again.
From chairs and stones, too, let the voice speak,
the cry of male and female shifting focus.
And when eye's liquor fills a clouded sky,
let it proclaim one unbounded, an I
undivided, that persists a joyous both.

Bring gifts then.
Place garlands around the pedestal, and
flowers there — yes, irises. And noiselessly
lay free the thresholds of your inner homes,
bring water,
above all high harvestings of thought,
now see — the god revives.
Raising from ecstasies of sleep an ebon flank
towards filtrating day, it will reveal
mysteries . . .

THE IMPORTANCE OF GAELIC

(1)
Just as what has been
vilified, guilt-ridden, repressed,
stowed away as shameful, condemned
on all sides, and almost forgotten,
lives on only as our hidden, inner,
unadmitted fantastic world,
that you have and I have
yet both pretend not to have:
that nut, kernel, vortex
gathered to itself force and violence
for the regeneration of the psyche,
for the renewal of the whole organism —
so for communities, nations and peoples
we must measure the significance of a way of life
not by its extent or its survival,
least of all by its success,
but by the nature of the opposition it provoked.

(2)
Even if we cannot bring back Gaelic
even if we wanted to bring back Gaelic
which in Scotland was never spoken
by more than three hundred thousand —
must we always talk with words intruded upon us,
not with those our mouths are naturally suited to form?
Will those who come after us
gaze dumb at an outstretched map
tracing the far off lines of distant hills
unable to say the name of even one?
How long are we to continue being
supereducated illiterates of our own culture?

(3)
When will we realise that culture
is about relationships between people,
that every time I cross a hill
a mother fondles her daughter,
father dandles her somehow differently.
chanting a different nonsense as they run the bath?
Books and universities are merely secondary.
Imperialism and capitalism can only
fagocitate our culture, they've no place for it.
No English lens can catch a Scottish scene.

(4)
I used to read Donald Macleod on the Clearances
with much passion, yet less, thinking:
'These people are gone, have left
no monument, scarce any vocal complaint
of what they suffered, and in Scotland
everyone has national insurance and free school dinners.
The important battles have been won after all.'
Not realising we pay a price
for every historical defeat
and that this one is especially heavy.
We pay for those evictions
with a dumbness below the level of consciousness,
a lebotomy of thought and of affections
that is crippling us still, now.

IF ONLY

If only I had, like Janacek, a country to be proud of:
a land that has hung on desperately to its culture
despite being crushed under the heels of Germand, Austrians and Russians
— or that at least, if it forgot its language for a while,
had the strength to recreate it and to produce again;
that even now finds people — journalists and playwrights —
who to defend rights and expressions will stand trial and go to prison
uselessly (they know their sacrifice won't change things).
The Czechs are only two or three millions more than the Scots.
And what have we got to be proud of?
Our landscape — a lot we did to create that!
Lakes and hills and red deer,

vast stretches of glen with no people to be seen,
and a land mass so equitably distributed among the population!
Our resilient sheep (and where from? not from Scotland)
are destroying the landscape as fast as they can.
We can't forget our language, our culture, our history
quick enough: they'll be remembered and their relicts studied
as Harvard University and in Central Europe
long after they have been completely forgotten
in Scotland.
Most Scots are too foolish to realise that just as the Czechs are important for us
so we are equally important for the Czechs!
We could be proud of our religious tolerance,
the absence of bigotry and divisiveness in our cities,
of having been the first to invent
corrupt, perennial and nepotistic local councils.
The trouble is, no intelligent Scotsman
can afford to be patriotic.
She — or he — has to find a substitute for patriotism.

Christopher Whyte

IAN STEPHEN

POET AND HARPER

fleur-de-lis on the fire-surrounds.
nothing burning in the hearth.
oatmeal-shaped board as a block.

backwall of velveteen decor.
a foreground body, shaped.
hair straight as harpstrings;

fingering shifting with fast care.
an ageing poet stands by for
incantation of a minority language.

no peat or Lothian coal
but fiercer heat than embers
could ever produce.

what makes the lines strong?
an adolescence of energy
in a stormy co-existence

with hours of skill, but he
had greatness in inexperience.
so did the mother of the harper:

the Barra woman with phrasing
that yet vibrates the ions
from Colonsay to Cape Wrath.

daughters re-learn the clarsach.
translators disseminate signs
but not on billboards.

outside the West End hotel
John Cooper Clerk is the name
on walls, halls, tickets.

Yevtushenko, they say, recited in
soccer stadiums, packed with the public.
but in the wake of this bardic evening

the late-night litter squad in
primary, quilted safety-jackets
collects cans and cartons below

floodlit turreted assets,
to the revving monoxide
of unsilenced exhausts.

COMMUNIST PARTY PRESS

the type set in frozen
red ink, advertising a
secular bazaar in Clydebank

on the 50's equivalent
of A5 size. the C.P.
press he'd run by hand.

she minded well her father
elected to speed to the Borders
to collect the speaker, who

they said had a reputation for
rhythms and lyrics as well as libel.
he wasn't very big to see,

nothing but shock-tactic hair
and no decorations but
a small, sunken moustache.

a transmission of upgoing awe,
carried by phrasing and woodbine
to their squat on the landing.

back to the selfsame stair
maybe a month or two ago,
her father gifted her the works.

lapsed memberships these days.
only rust seized presses.
he'd replace the fousted rollers

so she could print what she fancied
so long as it was the 50's
equivalent of A5 size.

ABSCONDING

a wind-storm in this day for work.
i flee the buff folders and the
billowing files as the warm

gale rebounds on my window.
inertia can be kick-started.
dryness in tyre-track and turf.

roaming along the single-track,
bypassing the mainstreams of cutters,
a teeming of bending and heaving:

the opening seams and the draining
channels; the scooped ditches.
this engine's own impulse

takes me to Morag the weaver.
she leaves her responsible tweed.
we abscond to the Viking mill.

we are idle as its paddles,
breezy as its rafters,
stilled as its slack querns.

then to the cross-currents of Dalmore.
we stumble over an archaeologist,
a sifter of stones, bones, clays.

she rubs with her horn-skinned fingers
for miniscule traces of Neolithic lives.
she distrusts that this settlement

is shored against tonight's tide,
a high spring with onshore gusting.
we cannot enter her burrow

but are impelled by the beckoning
of those who knew to rope
us to a promised hour.

Ian Stephen

RICHARD FLETCHER
Three Poems for E.C.M.

UNST WINTER

From Flugga to the Pole
is ocean, only ocean.

The geese flew south too soon.
On Hallows' Eve the gales
backed northerly and dew
made icicles that shivered
when roof-ropes twanged. Frost rimed
the weighting-stones, spades clanged
in peat, the iron splintering.
The cutters blew their hands
and gossip was all
of this sudden winter.
The young men told of smacks
caught up in voes that creaked
and thickened, calving grey bergs
where ice made haar with ocean —
these they had seen trekking
to the skerries on crackling waves.
The girls scoffed such fishers' tales —
but the month turned and the ice
piled south and west, bearing its wrecks,
hanging them crazily
above the crofts at Scolla,
sport for the boys who clambered,
hacked trophies from the floes,
cones of Norway spruce,

net shards, wrack of boxes.
But when they got other trove —
seals in bottle-cauls, sleek
as if summer basking,
and a sledge-dog tongue stiff lolling —
eyes turned from troubled eyes.
At solstice when they hauled
the first ewes home, stiff-fleeced
the old men thumbed their caps,
stamped threshholds, spat,
said — after all the crops were clamped,
peats stacked, plenty to last out
any winter. Such cold's
not Nature's way and the year's end
must see a change in things —
So they smoked, handed the bowl,
poked up their fires' cold glaze and dozed

while the wind droned
from the planet's grinding cap
sinewed with spits of ice that made
the sun a shrouded moon.
Stars burned against black

and the wells froze. Then the wives
shuddered from more than cold,
shawled their babes close and stared
in a terrible surmise
where the great spread arrowheads
of birds had gone.

The peat fires died,
first one, then one, and one.

IN YOUR OWN WORDS

Four vowels compose her name —
say *deft*, say *kiss, dance, death* —
like smoke rings, linked
exemplars of her faculty,
her advocacy and her carnal grammars.

To formulate the margins of her eyes,
four steps to duskfall, moonfall snared
to mirror her momentum and her style —
say *topaz, amber, auburn, black* —
her lip and boyish shoulder, archer's stance,
and one impatient gesture of disdain,
an earlobe tethered in a straying curl.
Laughable? Now say *charm*, say *warm, was warm.*

Or perhaps subsume her
in four fragrances, like dialects
abandoned but still braiding
here with then — *orchid, Havana,
Lentherique, quinine* — to wrench the noose,
affirm and reaffirm her.

Nothing is planned or willed or made
inevitable — *ever,* say *is it ever?* —
even by chance, by one-too-many faces
in a room — but somewhere
leaves ash to smoulder
as she left scents on gowns, in cars —
whisper *October,* whisper *smoke* and *gold* —
forsook her shoes by doors left open —
say *go, don't go, grown old* —
or charred the lips of unfamiliar tables
with her frank, familiar,
discarded black cigars.

GLASGOW HERO

The years her soul has wasted in her fate
whiten her knuckles on the witness rail
while the fiscal sifts her litany.
Others will cry her traitor, women not least.
'Put her ane man inside. Wee whooer!
What passed behind their door's no business
of Goad Almighty big-wigs, jugged and scarlet,
judging him hard man, beast and drunkard.'
His fists' tattoo earns him no more years than she
got broken teeth. They take him down,
hissing he'll have the bitch for this days lies,
curdling his hate. But when Court stands, she cries.

She finds something still in bloom in time —
enough to get her men in South Side bars
and for the dancing she experiments with wigs,
buys make-up and her first perfume
since the wedding-day
                            while he
slops out, dresses and undresses,
picks at his torment round the narrow yard,
writhes to her Judas touch each night
and waits — at her stairhead, or outside The Hauf.

Seven days freed he finds her, clacking her close
in gilded sling-backs some admirer gave.
He tips her face. 'Well, pet? His fond, sick smile's
a weapon, five years sharpened.
His knuckles tighten in her sacheted hair.
A blade slicks orange in the bare bulb's gloom
and there's the old, streaming fear —
'Christ! Naw, Shug — Naw!'
His stretch has drawn him keen, beyond imploring.
He razors her. Each kiss redeems one year.

Richard Fletcher

GEORGE BYATT

FISH FINGERS
OR — THE PREDICAMENT OF THE SCOTTISH PLAYWRIGHT

The proposition that a new and vital Scottish Theatre based on new writers and new writing had emerged in the last ten years seemed self evident not so long ago. The Great Northern Welly Boot Show of 1972 can be taken as the starting point of this development. But, it is now equally self evident that all is not as it should be.

The Predicament: — the Glasgow Citizen's Theatre continues to add to its European reputation without saying anything of any consequence about, or for, Scotland. The new Tron Theatre in Glasgow contributes to the long history of our cultural colonisation by appointing a duopoly of artistic directors from the very source of the colonialism — England. At the Royal Lyceum Theatre in Edinburgh, the Leslie Lawton Gang Show continues to gives us the same old tired programme of faded Broadway and West End 'hits'. Like the Citizens', but in different ways, it has a programme that could be equally at home in Watford or Weston-Super-Mare. The Traverse Theatre, the root of the whole Fringe theatre movement in the so-called British Isles, has moved far from its avant-grade beginnings. After a period of partial commitment to new Scottish writing, it seems to have moved into a new phase that has not yet crystallised. Elsewhere in Scotland, Perth, Dundee and Pitlochry, — with minor variations, continue to bend the same suppliant knee to Broadway and the West End as does the Lyceum.

A limited amount of tokenism towards new Scottish writing exists, but not enough in any of the above theatres to alter the overall impression that none of them are in Scotland. They seem rather to exist in some cultural cul-de-sac of the middle-class, middle-brow mind. And an English mind at that. The Citizens' is no exception to the rule. It is simply a quirky, up-market version of the status quo.

Thus the predicament of the Scottish playwright lies in the nature of what might be called, without too much irony, the 'commanding heights' of the Scottish Theatre. For at those rarified oxygen-starved heights there is, as far as can be judged, no vision. There is no vision of the theatre as a place where the vital issues of our culture can be explored; no awareness that the theatre should be the people talking to themselves; not a hint that Scottish culture is still a vital oral culture and that the theatre is the natural high point of social communication in such a culture. To be fair none of these ideas may have occurred to those responsible for running these theatres. That is, if it is fair to accuse them of crass, mind-bending, bewildering ignorance of their own cultural context and the way in which they relate to it. Or, as in the case in question, the way they *fail* to relate to it. For most of them, the anal count, or 'bums on seats' as they indelicately put it, is the index of theatrical success. There's vision for you.

The Monopoly game: apart from the lack of vision of the theatres is the problem of their limited number. Because of this they constitute an artistic monopoly and act as a built-in barrier to future development. None of them has the kind of studio theatre in which new writing can have a place to try and triumph. Or, equally important, fail. True, there existed for short periods of time, such places as the Close Theatre in Glasgow and the Young Lyceum in Edinburgh. Fire destroyed the first, and what looked like a sword destroyed the second. Both parent companies seem relieved rather than distressed at the premature deaths of their not-quite legitimate children.

Outside of the theatres mentioned, there are what we might call the theatres without a theatre, the touring companies. The two largest of these at the moment are the 7:84 company and its music orientated offspring — Wildcat Theatre. To 7:84 belongs the honour of pioneering a new kind of touring company in Scotland — politically orientated and populist. Wildcat is in a related mould. But despite 7:84's recent re-kindling of Scottish popular plays of the Forties, neither company is able to offer much opportunity to writers other than those who are already members of their respective organisations. This is not a criticism, but simply notes a fact that is the result of the origins and histories of both companies. Nevertheless the Scottish playwright's predicament proliferates.

A death worse than fate: but suppose for a dreadful moment that one of the 'commanding heights' theatres did decide to produce a play by a new Scottish writer. What fate would await the writer's work? Not, surely, a fate worse than death? No — worse. Just the death of the play as the writer has conceived it, and this because all of these establishments operate on the same hierarchical model as the Broadway and West End which they ape. They employ a director, usually male, to 'direct' the play. This is to say that an authority figure re-interprets the writer's work to fit the theatrical pre-conceptions of the status quo. The idea that the writer could produce the play in conjunction with the actors is met with amused and patronising contempt. Such an attitude is of course completely ahistorical. The director as we know him, and I use 'him' deliberately, is a product of nineteenth century naturalism (the pretence that the actors are 'real' people talking to each other, unaware of the presence of the audience. This is the prevailing mode in the 'commanding heights', a mode that comes trailing clouds of unexamined social and political implications. The director is the blind servant of this mode.

Perhaps the best way to illustrate the handling of a play in such circumstances is to tell a story: — and it came to pass that a playwright went forth to fish with rod and line. For days, weeks, months, years, a lifetime even, the writer patiently waited for a tug on the line that dipped into the limpid pool of the collective unconscious. Finally, there was a ripple on the surface, and after an exhausting but exciting tussle, a great, gleaming, living, silver fish was landed. Then, still living, still struggling, it was presented to a theatre.

Ah, we too are excited, the theatre said. This is the most beautiful fish we have ever seen. See how silver it is. See how it turns and twists. Above all, it delights. This one will twist and turn and turn forever. Lo. Behold. Here is your director. He will, with your approval of course, choose your actors. And he will show your fish to all the people. And so the director did take the fish, and, with his chosen actors, at his behest, and accepting his wisdom and with great effort, they did kill that great, living, silver fish. And they did turn it into fish fingers. And then they held them up for all the people to see.

Woe. Woe.

Some writers and most directors might dispute the truth of this story. Many playwrights will recognise its bitter relevance to their own experience and it may go some way to explain the failed promise of new Scottish writing in the seventies. It's fair of course to say that writers in other cultures have the same kind of problem.

The fringe that grew: in England in the late sixties and into the seventies there was a related upsurge of new theatre writing. This upsurge did fulfill its promise in a spectacular way. Taking their cue from the Edinburgh Festival fringe and from the pioneering work of the original Traverse Theatre in the Lawn market, low budget theatres appeared in pub rooms and basements in many parts of London. The Soho Poly theatre, founded in 1969 by the late Verity Bargate and Fred Proud is perhaps the best known and most successful example. Through this tiny basement theatre went, and still goes, some of the best and freshest writing and acting talent in the whole of England. Other small theatres like the Bush and the King's Head also continue to flourish. Around them, a stream of such theatres live and die and are sometimes re-born. New writers in London have some hope of performance, while here in Scotland there is almost none.

This London Fringe or Alternative theatre altered the direction of the mainstream. Today many of its writers now have plays performed in their 'commanding heights' — the West End, The National, The Royal Shakespeare and The Royal Court. Whether this has been a good thing or a bad thing is a matter for debate. They have directors in abundance in England and they also make fish fingers. In Scotland there never has been an Alternative theatre in the London manner, and because of this lack, the seventies upsurge of writing here was absorbed directly into the fish finger industry.

No way out or round or through? To summarise then — there are too few theatre outlets in Scotland. Their monopoly constitutes a barrier to developing writing talent and the values they live by are more likely to destroy new talent rather encourage it. Where then can the playwright, new and established, turn to? Is there, as H.G. Wells once said in another context, no way out or round or through?

Fortunately, a way out is emerging for Scottish Playwrights in the eighties. Soon there may be ways round and through. The way out is the Workshop movement now beginning to expand here. The best example of this kind of theatre in Scotland is the Edinburgh Playwrights' Workshop. Founded three years ago by writers, actors and others, the EPW has been running regular programmes of new writing by writers both new and old. Each play in the series has a deliberately restricted rehearsal period (to keep as close to the original text as possible). Each is presented, script in hand, by professional actors to a public audience. There are no sets or costumes and no light changes. Props are minimal or non-existent. Where possible, the plays use a limited amount of movement. Plays presented in this way have to be good to survive and the survival rate among these plays is an index of the strength and quality of a body of new works that cry out for production. More than fifty plays have been presented by the EPW in this way in the last three years. No other professional theatre group in Scotland, and possibly in England, can lay claim to such an output. The plays have ranged from the reworking of a neglected early seventeenth century verse play to contemporary plays about oil rig workers. There have been many others of different style and content in between. Radio, television as well as theatre plays are included in this programme. Several plays have gone on to production but not as many as could do so. In every case the writer concerned has been primarily responsible for their presentation. Ideally this is done in full and free collaboration with the actors involved.

After each presentation, the plays are discussed by audience, actors and writers. The discussions are structured so that all present are given an opportunity to comment if they wish. These discussions are seen as an essential part of the whole process. The weekly 'anal' count at the time of writing is between forty and fifty and is on the increase.

The initial workshops were financed from their own box office returns. Later the Scottish Society of Playwrights gave its support. And now the Scottish Arts Council provide a minimal budget for what could become the Scottish Alternative Theatre of the near future. The critic Joyce MacMillan has described the workshops in Scottish Theatre News as 'a completely new form of theatrical event ... cheap, informal, immediate and heavily dependent on audience participation ... their contribution to theatrical life in Edinburgh has already been substantial.' The EPW are committed to the work of writers mainly based in the capital, but their declared aim is to encourage other Scottish cities and centres to set up their own similar enterprises. Surely, here are the seeds of the future?

Alternatives: but after the way out, where is the way round and through? It is not provident to be too specific about coming developments. They will take their own course based on the initial impetus derived from the workshops. Already several new production companies have emerged in Edinburgh and more than one has put workshop plays into full professional production. All these companies are based on the work of particular writers. Theatre Vortex has Christina Johns as its writer. Rona Munro is the writer for Stage Traffic and Border Reivers is Howard Purdie's company. Older established companies such as Mental Guerrillas and Theatre PKF are in close contact with the new companies. And new works by the writers George Gunn, Katy Gardiner and Rob Laing are being planned for production. Other companies in Edinburgh and Glasgow are also consciously or unconsciously part of what begins to look like a new phase in the life of the theatre in Scotland. In a matter of months rather than years, we should begin to see results that will show the way round and through.

It is an exciting prospect for everyone, writers, actors and audience. The river is full of living silver fish. The banks are crowded with fisherpersons. There is a growing awareness that co-operation and not competition is the real law of life. Scotland is small enough and big enough to create a new theatre that could take its place in Europe and the World. If we go about it all in the right way the predicament of the Scottish playwright could disappear. An Alternative theatre could take us round the 'commanding heights' and who knows, the fish finger industry might itself be led to find new values to live by. But that's a story for the future, one that many of us look forward to writing.

George Byatt

J. MAXWELL HASTIE

SOME OBSERVATIONS ON HOW THE SCOTS DEFINE THEMSELVES WITH A VIEW OF THE NATIVE PHILOSOPHY

The ensuing remarks are not intended to trespass upon the domain of such specialist publications as *The Scottish National Dictionary,* Dwelly's *Gaelic-English Dictionary,* Johnnie Gibb's *Gushetneuk* or Baxter's *Parliamo Glasgow.* I merely wish to inform our English or foreign visitors of certain usages which are common throughout the Lowlands, Borders and most tracts of English-speaking Highlands and Islands.

HOW SCOTSMEN DEFINE EACH OTHER

A Braw Bugger[1] One who can shite[2] with the best of them.
1. The term 'bugger' when applied by one Scots man to another has no sexual significance, even in sheep rearing parishes. Since to the Scot a man is the highest form of created life, to call a man 'a man' is to overpraise him.
2. The male Scots prefers excretion to sexuality because although both are equally inevitable, the first is less expensive.

A Dour Bugger One who can't shite yet refuses to take the medicine.

A Thrawn Bugger One who can't shite, takes the medicine yet still refuses to shite.

A Canny Bugger One who can't shite, takes the medicine, still can't shite, returns the medicine and his money is refunded.

An Uncanny Bugger One who can't shite, takes the medicine, won't shite, returns the medicine, has his money refunded — then shites!

Note that the Braw Bugger and the Uncanny Bugger, the alpha and omega of this spectrum, have a common characteristic — their bodily functions are unimpeded by moral imperatives.

THE SCOTS AND THEIR PROPERTY

The Scots, like many deprived races, have a passionate attachment to the basic essentials of food, drink and slumber, which they underline by their frequent deployment of the personal pronoun:

eg. *Do you want a bit of my fish?*
You'll have had your tea?
I'm going home to my bed.

However, the male Scot's lack of all proprietorial instinct towards the female will gladden the hearts of the most ardent feminists. It is shown in his preference of the indefinite article over the personal pronoun when identifying his spouse, actual or intended.

eg. *No thanks, I'm going home to the wife.*
No thanks, I'm going out with the bird.

Contrariwise, the acquisitive and rapacious attitude of the average Scots woman towards the male counterpart is nowhere more evident than in her heavy-handed insistence of the personal pronoun:

eg. *My man kicked hell out of me last night.*
It's aff his Da my boy gets his nae brains frae.
My fiance's done a bunk again.

SCOTTISH POSITIVISM, THE PERENNIAL PHILOSOPHY

Scratch a Scot and you will find a philosopher. Scottish philosophical thought is so deeply engrained in the national psyche that the works of Hume, Hamilton, Carlyle and Horatio McTeague must be regarded as mere outcroppings of the native bedrock, whose quality is best revealed in the following dicta, which may be heard in any laundrette, turf accountant's office or football changing room:

What's for ye will no go past ye — The world is all that is the case. (Is-ness is all; is replaces if).

It'll aa be the same hunner years frae noo — In that the past is irremediable, any finite point in the future will display the same charateristics.

It'll no be this in the mornin — Since the present is tolerable, it is highly unlikely that a finite point in the future will display the same characteristics.

This by no means comprehends the extant. Further observation may well yield fruits.

J. Maxwell Hastie

RAYMOND J. ROSS
EDINBURGH
(For Sorley MacLean)

City of crags and hills,
Of gardens, ponds and lochs,
City of castles and meadows,
Palace and Mound,
You are noted in the Annals of Europe
For your Folly.

City of Knox and Mary,
City of Enlightenment,
Europe has a catalogue
Of your history and pretensions.
Your history cannot assuage
The poverty and bitterness of Pilton,
And Craigmillar stands ashamed
Before its castle.

ROBERT CALDER

THE QUESTIONS CONCERNING SCOTTISH CIVILISATION

(Sir James) Steuart at once reminds us of our obligations ... and invites us to take out ideas and concepts which have become part of the furnishing of our minds. To do this we must think about ideas, and perhaps this is the lesson which Steuart desired, above all else, to teach.

One can imagine that G.E. Davie chose to call his book *The Democratic Intellect* for good reason. That title certainly means something, isn't only a handy label hatched of a need to find that book some name. Part of what that title seems to refer to is caught by Andrew Skinner's above-quoted comment about a notable Jacobite and Presbyterian thinker, one into whose intellectual resources Sir Walter Scott may not have had much insight. Steuart came forward to proclaim to his countrymen the continuing, inherent superiority of the Continental ideal: a conscious inwardness satisfied with nothing short of a holistic view, honest with detail, not simply filled out with crayon of optimism. Left, if maybe not behind, by Adam Smith and others embracing simpler ideas of post-Union economic advance, Steuart's case offers evidence of virtues of breadth and length of view which hint at certain problems posed for culture by a bias toward simplification and optimism. To be optimistic and cleave to simplicity biasses thinking at the expense of deeper examination. That slant, Enlightenment but not Scottish, has perhaps been a major one in undermining the country's culture, from within as from without.

Certainly *The Democratic Intellect* does not refer to some *age d'or* of Scottish culture, as championed by some commentators today. Indeed several simplifier-mystifiers could be impeached for a decadent inconsistency. Belief in such an age, pre-anglicisation or whatever, sits ill among those who fail to think, write, in accord with the lights a scholarly criticism reveals as essential to the historical period on which the fable is based. If Empedokles believed in a golden age when men ate no meat, and envisaged its restoration, he at least ate no meat. No such fastidiousness of critical intelligence redeems those who have sought to fabulise Dr. Davie's book to lip-serve *or minimise* it. Dr. Davie is not to be confused with his book's fleas. He does not follow the habitual rules of thumb which comfort numbers of historians either; more than most, he knows what he is doing.

The argument of *The Democratic Intellect* at once rejects two popular misconceptions which mislead in any account of history: the first is that the past influences simply some 'hair of midnight' present, and that that present is what influences the future. The second is one which dangerously pervades writings and readings of history in academic History, historical novels and novels of a recognisably historical context. That misconception is implied by a thinking which in effect excludes a possibility of criticising the present; of disguising a restriction of human intelligence, critical or imaginative, as some 'art of the possible'. The restriction is presumably a rule of thumb to discountenance misuse of historical material by the ilk of aforementioned *fleas*. It would be a sorry pass were such a restriction finally to render the historian incapable of debate involving ideas.

Such a failure was plain when Professor Smout wrote his introduction to the reissue of Edwin Muir's *Scottish Journey*. There he pursued a policy of looking for imperfections in what MacDiarmid had written; aided by a deplorable practice of parodying those ideas at times drastically in the course of summarising them, he turned them into sitting ducks and potted them. Or rather he potted his convenient misrepresentations — voodoo dolls?

As C.S. Peirce remarked of J.S. Mill's attack on Sir William Hamilton (cited by Davie) 'he wants to root out this philosophy by adequate arguments or inadequate ones.'

The trouble with all such displays of military hardware is that they leave imperfect ideas without a possibility of refinement into more interesting form. The ideas are not criticised at all! What dies is no party or body of ideas, but the very question and possibility of debate. If one grants that Dr. Davie has exposed much of the detail of what befell the Scottish universities and their ideals during the Nineteenth century, Professor Smout's errors may offer some clear analogy, even if he was confronted with a more deliberately provocative figure in MacDiarmid. But what precisely is the relevance of Dr. Davie's book beyond the history of educational institutions?

What died or declined undiscussed? To that question an answer is required involving some account of the history of Scottish culture, indeed of the nature of what could be called Scottish culture, even *civilisation*.

Such an account must record a widespread contemporary ignorance, bred of a secular bias, of the sheerly practical importance and value to Scotland's history of the church's element of culture. When Edwin Muir remarked that the best minds in Scotland had for a long time gone into science and technology, or had in the humanities expressed themselves strictly via the church and established institutions, he said a lot. Not being of so decadent a cast of mind as to be interested in a poetry that turns its back on all but feeling, we might see in that something quite apart from any dismissal of tracts of history as barren.

Certain concerns integral to anybody's humanity, and to a scrupulous and intelligent literature, were in Scotland borne by the church direct, or by the related universities. If today's kirk and universities command no or little adherence among some litterateurs and intellectuals, and do not carry the weight of these concerns either, perhaps one valuable part of the task is not being done at all. Which may have something to do with the widespread slightness and shallowness of modern Scottish literature. Perhaps the absence of intelligent literary criticism might be related to poetry's current want of the sort of interest which could satisfy a good critical mind?

As the period of the Scottish Enlightenment opened, neither the church nor the universities Dr. Davie discusses were as they are today, to say nothing of poetry. Church and university were in the Eighteenth century integral to Scottish society, which cannot be said without another emphasis: Scottish society and culture could not but have been very different from what they have been of late, when institutions of general and intellectual concern were not *in* the country so much as part of its overall texture. To recognise certain laming features consequent on church hegemony is not however to see that as simply a set of chains to be shed. If one cannot look squarely at Scottish Neocalvinism and observe its virtues, one's general critical abilities must be in doubt.

The questions concerning anglicisation: In a *caveat* uttered in 1968, when the SNP was showing some renewal of vigour, William Ferguson qualified his bibliographical reference to G.E. Davie's *The Democratic Intellect* as follows: 'Davie ... attributes the decline and fall (of Scotland's university culture) to anglicising influences, but his views have not been generally accepted. The change may, in fact, merely have denoted a transition to a technological age.' *(Scotland since 1689)*

Following the practice of Norman Kemp Smith and John MacMurray, two Edinburgh philosophy professors of great breadth and far more than specialist interest, one should look at that statement according to what has been called the historical method in philosophy. What was the historian saying to 1968, what to 1983?

The unusual question can be a revealing one, especially with such a brief and I should say hasty *caveat* as the above, since one assumes the historian's somewhat muddled statement is an attempt to say something worth saying. One cannot merely attack it without seeing what its author may have been trying to say. The attack on it is not a defence of *The Democratic Intellect* but a plain recognition of the defects of thinking embodied in the statement.

The question concerning that *caveat* has to do with what 'anglicisation' can mean. What is it?

Certainly in 1968 it was a highly charged term, liable to be used very carelessly as a slogan meaning something bad. There I think lies the force of the *caveat:* the dutiful historian is bound to contest any attempt to manipulate history's material evidence to serve a political cause. Such dishonest and unhistorical conduct is at the heart of what passes for intellectual activity under totalitarian regimes, Soviet, Nazi, whatever. It is to be doubly condemned as dangerously dishonest, abetting bad government and the misuse of power, propaganda and lies. Were the historian's statement cogent and acceptable, one could see it as a criticism of the book, and also — what it certainly is — a dutiful attempt to discourage the book's fleas. Fleas, those who draw from books and persons only the sustenance required to sustain their very limited existences — were not uncommon in the late 1960's surge of pro-SNP enthusiasm. In cultural terms they might be seen as English liberals, seeking to find some good cause in which to ground and discharge impulses of a moral sort. Certainly they had nothing, many of them, of the resolve to 'distrust simplicity' which G.E. Davie I think rightly regards as an essential of Scottish Culture. Culturally also, their rejection of 'anglicisation' might be seen not as a relation to England specifically, but simply as parochialism of a sort, an intellectually narrow exclusiveness which Edwin Muir identified as a central and sustaining feature of what was wrong with Scottish Calvinism at a certain period — and indeed with post — Cromwellian England, where a conviction crude as that 'we are right' can be seen accepted as justification for colonialist and economic practices allied to a missionary zeal. How many in the 1960's SNP said nothing but by way of uttering excuses for the belief 'we are right'? I am trying to indicate that the dutiful historian's *caveat* was addressed to a very anglicised version of what 'anglicisation' means.

Alas he falls short by a long way of representing what G.E. Davie actually says, as what seems by its title a most unattractive part of *The Democratic Intellect* shows well. I refer to the chapters on the fate of the Scottish tradition of mathematics teaching. Certainly what happened there, more solidly substantiable than Dr. Davie's brilliant account of possible lines of resistance to the imposition of uniformity with Cambridge — that account is qualified in an exemplary manner — was that imposition of uniformity. Yet the intellectual, theoretical stimuli within mathematical work which conduced to that imposition, were not from English but from continental sources. The changes could be called anglicising only in a larger, more detailed sense than was at all current in SNP discourse — and than strikes the eye in the wording of that *caveat*. In fact to see that is to grasp something of what is wrong with that *caveat,* if reference to a 'technological age' has not already affronted the reader.

It would have affronted Edwin Muir, who puts the matter very plainly: to speak of a necessary transition from one sort of age to another, so that previous all-embracing moral and cultural traditions are no longer practicable, is to deny human agency. Men are seen, in terms of such historicist transitions, as sheerly the material of nature's adaptive, impersonal, inhuman forces. That is quite what Dr. Ferguson implies when he reduces the question of Scottish cultural decline — the sacrifice of certain intellectual ideals — to the sort of rule-of-thumb phrase he uses. Elsewhere, Dr. Ferguson is very clear that he does see quite what a ragbag of ill-assorted elements the Scottish M.A. syllabus of the '60s had become, and he is free of the sort of mechanical historicism which deforms Scottish work too often. This use of his hasty note by me is somewhat opportunistic, and I apologise to him for it. Nevertheless he has chanced to put a popularised or 'flea's' point of view very usefully.

The Scottish tradition's being surrendered to Cambridge mathematics may seem somewhat out of the way, but at first glance so might a book that could superficially be taken for a study in the history of Scottish universities. Why is *The Democratic Intellect* of any general relevance? I re-emphasise: to an extent almost unthinkable today, the universities were not simply *in* Scotland but part of the texture of a distinctive and valuable culture which extended right across the country, where church and school influences, and access to and interest in books, were real.

Insight into the nature of this culture is hampered by againan oversimplistic rejection of the church and what the church and its moderate and other clergy did as an element governing and informing Scotland before, during and after the period of the Scottish Enlightenment. Mr. P.H. Scott would have us believe that the ideals of the Scottish Enlightenment are embodied in easily digestible form in the homogenised works of Sir Walter Scott — although he reinforces the impression that he does not know what he is talking about when he refers simply to 'Enlightenment'. He also implies something authoritaian when he confuses the books of Scott — by his way of speaking — with those of the Author of Nature.

The reforming Renaissance Calvinism of the great Latinist Andrew Melville's day bequeathed to Scotland an inestimably valuable focus, a fruitful tension between a mediaeval concern for the whole and a prescribed degree of conscious inwardness. The Calvinist system of Scotland ossified, arguments granted as right became no longer ground for exercise of thought — like the platitudinous statements of angloliberalism they were reduced to affairs of the memory, even if they stirred levels of thought and feeling likely in the end to challenge the parrotings as liberal platitudes and sophisms do not.

What was living in Scottish intellectual activity clove to elements of Continental thought, reviving Renaissance elements in connection with their European variants in the Aufklärung to generate a Scottish intellectual ideal of breadth of interest. That ideal included some concern with the question of *Man's* nature, although what had been half-dead in Scottish Calvinism made its return by the disruption of 1843 to divide the church and forfeit its elements of broad concern as a force governing the country. The legal establishment to some extent stressed practical advantage, the church has its own complex emphasis, made real by the power of that institution pover the universities and as a force in the land. With the disruption that force diminished, indeed sowed some dissension in the running of the universities and opended up a gulf between an educational ideal of inward, intellectual *plus* practical concern, and what can be called a kind of protest element subsequently very significant in Scottish life.

I refer to the deprived, in fact, starved population of industrial workers, whose lack of bread and estrangement from education bred no continuation of repesct for learning of the kind which at best gave Scotland an estimable awareness of a *docta ignorantia*. A man can be absolutely right when he affirms his knowledge that unless he eats he will die. He has an abiding and exclusive concern with economic improvement which can be justified where a well-fed utilitarian's can be questioned. But what is necessary and what is useful cannot be identified wholesale with what is adequate.

The Scottish tradition of disputation, fostered by the manner of university teaching in some areas, and by traditions of university societies in others, was with philosophy an element in what I have termed somewhat inadequately 'breadth'. It was rather more, emphasising the necessity of disputation, and of a philosophic concern for first principles, not for the sake of some good cause of 'the whole man' as conceived on angloliberal principles. The concern was to do justice to certain important affairs of human life. Disputation rather than the settling of questions, if it does not presume too hastily that questions *can* rather then *can't* be settled, is awareness of conflicting demands, moral and intellectual and social and religious. If philosophy is what brings a being to fuller humanity by enabling him to handle the enlivening problem of meeting these demands, philosophy's central position, is not one of autocratic power or authority. It is itself shaped no less and no more than shaping, by the task of avoiding bringing inappropriate first principles to bear on some specialised concern — or of avoiding applying the practical principles, rules of thumb, of a specialisation, illicitly to bear on a larger matter. What Wyndham Lewis called 'bad' nationalism could equally be termed algebraic nationalism. Structuralist writings on literature lapse not only into the mechanistic materialistic philosophy of the last century, but the Hobbesian philosophy whose overthrow by Hutcheson marked something of the real start of the Scottish philosophy.

Docta ignorantia: Dr. Davie cites H.T. Buckle's assertion that the Scots should have had the sense, as Buckle saw it, to slough off religous-metaphysical proccupations for the sake of attaining to practical, scientific and social objectives the Scots also coveted. Believing himself right, Buckle plainly had little time for the characteristic Scottish schema; the reflective relation of philosophy, as something both questioned and questioning, to him seemed an impedance. But what use is a straight line without direction?

The positivistic shedding of religion can seem simple, but is far from simple. To abandon religious beliefs may be one thing. That nevertheless carries with it the problem — mishandled by liberals — of tackling questions the church handled. What is the nature of the human creature?

The theological bias kept the questions of *man* alive. What or who is doing the work of challenging the alleged adequacy of an optimistic, quasi-scientific sense of damned rightness, in Scotland today? The church does not have its former, even provisional part in the fabric of Scottish culture. If it cannot ever, now, something must do that work, take that part.

One can, contra Nineteenth-century Misreadings of Man, apply a formula of *docta ignorantia* towards an understanding of Scottish culture in some general terms. If schooling could be bad or absent in places, MacDiarmids maybe ingloriously mute, an abiding respect for learning and thought does carry some prospect of being aware of one's ignorance. If it accompanies a desire to think and learn, one element of a general sort of democratic culture definitely exists.

Hugh Miller, a stonemason of no university's training, exemplifies not simply that, but something much more complex in detail, which bespeaks no mere possibility.

Miller was not only a *thinking* journalist of the evangelical party of the 1843 disruption, he was a very notable palaeontologist who impressed the Swiss Louis Agassiz at Harvard, in a very real sense teacher of C.S. Peirce, William James and Henry Adams. Miller possessed to a very high degree the spirit of disputation — which is also, so to speak, sceptical about scepticism. His education, classroom and pulpit, was mercifully free of that 'all you need to know' fallacy the *populariser* wears. The urge to get at truth was strong. More than did Darwin, Miller felt what Lorine Niedecker expressed in her poem about the great English naturalist and prose-writer:

> Species are not —
> it is like confessing a murder —
> immutable

Like Robertson Smith, the great pioneer of anthropology, Miller was a believing member of the Evangelical church party, not approximating to liberalism in theology. By concentrating not on change or adaptation but on form, morphology, Miller might be caricatured by a Buckle-ite as clinging to religious beliefs which hampered his thinking. But surely form does matter. Surely there is some principle in nature such that for instance Hugh Miller exists as observer. Consideration given to the detail of what has existed, and what exists, is an inevitable consequence of allowing that some things which exist — for instance, oneself — are not redundant.

Miller's thought is characteristic, indicative of an approach, a tendency, of a sort one finds as a structuring impulse where a substantial culture is at work. Neither the thought nor the tendency can be self-validating, nor can the conclusions be taken for granted, any more than their contradictory can be — or can be assumed somehow culture-free. Miller's ideas breed large-mindedness, concern for range and implication, when matched with a different cultural focus.

Left on its own, as German or another Kultur has sought to be, the general Scottish focus could deteriorate into something like the indigenous source from which it came, or into something perilously close to angloliberalism with its missionary zeal and its lack of thinking concern, species of parochialism. Miller confronted Darwin, Darwin had his facts, but as Maynard Smith and others now make plain the Englishman's easy gradualism (c.f. Sir Walter Scott) has an inadequacy not to be dissevered from thoughts of the focus of his culture.

But like Miller, Darwin preserved an immunity to the common blindnesses to evidence: denial of evidence, a flea-like drawing of a little blood from it. The Darwin Miller opposed was an image of the man made by his followers, one whose projection into cultural, human affairs Edwin Muir criticised acutely.

Discussing Clerk Maxwell, Davie clarifies much of the indigenous Scottish concern for practical matters which was fading into another approach by Maxwell's day, and which is not seen in its proper breadth today when the Scottish concern with science is half-remembered. Maxwell certainly showed all the features of not a nostalgic Scotticism but a resistance to that process whereby an easy efficiency converts a man of strong aptitude into a kind of sub-human or at least imperfecttly responsible functionary.

Muir's rugging at the profoundly practical, technological direction of the Scottish intelligence takes issue most, when you look at it, with that half-remembering. Yet Muir has some common cause with the Calvinist Humanist Melville too, where he struggled to budge the universities from a sterile, late-mediaeval torpor. No golden age then, in a society of considerable injustices where in the modern enfranchised view abuses of people would not be far to seek, whatever was hidden, and whatever commendable literature existed written and oral. Each age has things to offer against the wholesale description of it as black, golden, or lead, but it seems fair enough comment to wonder about the country which could fall so wholly under a Neocalvinist regimen. Outwith a close account, statements are as likely to conceal more than they reveal. Beyond its detail that regimen established a peculiarly useful balance between individuality and social responsibility that commands a critical not condemnatory approach.

But what of today? What of fear of totalitarianism, the Soviet Union, anglicisation? Genuine opposition to these ought surely to learn from the imposition of angloliberal onesidedness on Scotland: that what is of the essence is to identify and understand what should not and must not be lost. 'Better Red than Dead' does imply in a non-Communist a faith that the human spirit can outdo technology; but if corruption is preferable to obliteration, there is no guarantee that it is an alternative capable of ensuring that obliteration does not occur.

The Democratic Imagination: I offer Miller as exemplar of a democratic culture, practical intellectual activity of a high order *plus* strong inner concern with profound attention to spirituality. Outwith Science, the humanities have Hogg, Muir and MacDiarmid to offer, the latter obviously stressing science, as evidence of a Scottish democratic culture that endured into this century. Nurtured in proximity to what Buckle overstated as liberality in politics and illiberality in religion, the latter an excessive inwardness, potentially, these men give distinguished literary expression to claims of one Scottish culture. Strong claims of spirit, intellect, imagination and social concern dispute in terms unlikely to be harmonisable all into an oversimplified, blended lowest common denominator. The Scottish concrete awareness of where a via media is to be found can be contrasted with an angloliberal practice of trying to start from *how it feels* to be on it.

Such a broadening of reference may not be red into or from Davie's careful account of the Scottish ideals and values in decline in the universities. This provisional account is an attempt to suggest larger and perhaps unsuspected consequences, seeing the Scottish educational decline as a failure to grasp questions of an integration Edwin Muir missed by the time of *Scottish Journey.*

With Hogg certainly the precise intellectual formulation of *The Brownie of Bodsbeck* has long gone unremarked, along with observations of its form such that it approximates to the series of fireside tales rather than to a non-existent tradition of the Scottish novel. Hogg reinvented genres from native roots — *The Three Perils of Man* is an encyclopaedia. If Hogg was never any great shakes at expressing himself in the language of analysis, and he didn't impress Carlyle, perhaps the snobbery of Scott and company beat down his confidence.

The Brownie has much to say concerning the genesis of myth, and also (cf. Adam Smith) the stimulus to rational enquiry. The hero of *The Brownie* is informed by his fantastic experience. Hogg's satire of mud-stuck common sense raises questions of the necessary vivifying of the common-sense thinker which might have pressed Scott & Co. had they not been stuck in something more perfumed.

Hogg's *Sinner,* deriving force from its language's genesis in the catechised intellectual formulas of the religious literature, may even imply a respectable account of antique Neocalvinism. Perhaps that system was itself an unconscious parody of something intellectually important? Kemp Smith does note that hardly any intellectual system could be less amenable to an adequate popular representation than that of Calvin.

The *Sinner* brings out another crucial point, an English misconception of the nature of Scottish literature which W.E. Aytoun perpetuated, and which one recent lip-server of *The Democratic Intellect* lately encapsulated as 'it's a popular tradition'. As Davie decisively argues, the Scottish tradition has had as a crucial element that it was popular *plus* or incorporating intellectualism. Perhaps Hogg suffered for a confusion of the intelligent with the socially prestigious.

Prestige versus the value of human endeavour: In trying to round off this series of reflections drawn from a much larger work in progress, I cannot but be conscious that what I offer here has more suggestiveness than unity, that my business has been the awakening of questions rather than something that has bartered for either the systematic or the simple. I have not done justice to *The Democratic Intellect,* although I would hope to have at least quickened a reading of it.

The 'anglicising' of which the historian wrote would seem on analysis to demand not only a deeper examination — perhaps no less fruitful to those whose concern is with English culture — but probably a different name. I have here and there used the word angloliberal, not to impugn virtues of liberalism but to question the proceeding whereby some sophistical platitude — like 'moderation' — has been used with even less than moderate honesty to smother the course of rigorous argument. One recent writer of uneven scholarship suggests in his book that *The Democratic Intellect* errs in the direction of overstating the differences between the British (sic) and the Scottish universities, where Dr. Davie does not in fact venture any detailed comparison that would make that claim meaningful. He says little, either, of the English nonconformism whose scion A.R.Orage, great and neglected critic, fostered Muir's and MacDiarmid's gifts in the pages of his periodical *The New Age.*

There, in truth, the English too say little today, about congenial Englishmen who may subsequently have helped to arrest the decline of Scottish culture. The questions concerning Scottish culture concern principally what ought not to be lost, and what causes that to be lost. A larger perspective would ideally consider the concurrent English decline too, and would one presumes come to related conclusions.

The Cambridge mathematical focus may be seen as weaving together continental influences in a culturally determind way, no less than when Hugh Miller gathered his material and arguments. In saying that Cambridge was influenced by an inferior culture, I am not being nationalist; surely some critique of English culture — uncomfortable in adherence to *any* political party — must be part of an account of Scottish. Anglophobia and Anglophilia are both necessary, together, and to any Englishman too.

At root the 'anglicisation' may indeed be a variant of something bigger, international if perhaps of German origin, as criticised by various 'Questions concerning Technology'. Thinking on the biochemist Steven Rose's continuing arguments against the philosophical, dehumanising fallacies implicit in current laboratory practice, some of the greater worth of Dr. Davie's book may inhere in its clarifying questions too long unasked — and necessary to be asked again. What a 'technological age' deems redundant may be only the necessary critique of that age. As the recently dead English poet Ronald Duncan wrote, in *Man,* a poem tackling the subject-matter of science:

the notion that if there are two alternatives,

and one is wrong, then it follows the other is correct:

recipe for idiocy ...

The human dilemma

Is where we are. Optimism, form of vanity;

pessimism, form of conceit.

In the end it may be that what has undermined Scottish culture has been that peculiarly noxious form of optimism which cankers the body politic and perpetrates abuses by taking as its objective nothing but the very increase in optimism *qua* optimism.

The meaning of the title *The Democratic Intellect* broadens beyond Scotland's boundaries to state that democracy can make sense only where the enfranchised person is educated and thinking, has a method rather than a doctrine, an apparatus of the mind, a technique of thinking. The possibility of that may be the only ground for any optimism, though such an approach to reality ought to make dowy thoughts of optimism superfluous.

The Democratic Intellect, highlighting possibilities in their hour of perhaps death, indicates that Scotland need not perhaps be 'functionless' in the terms of Edwin Muir's essay, *The Functionlessness of Scotland.* Not it, not any book or possibility, can guarantee that Scotland is not and will not be functionless. What may be the case need not be the case, seems the merest truism. I wish it were less apt. Like any valuable book, *The Democratic Intellect* is to be commended less than what it commends; also, it implies criticism of those who praise as those who dispraise it. But I wish the commendably economical production had been matched with an equally praiseworthy price. Current book-prices are another question concerning Scottish civilisation.

The Democratic Intellect by G.E. Davie; Edinburgh University Press, paperback £10.00.

Robert Calder